Collins

AQA GCSE 9-1
Food Preparation and Nutrition

Revision Guide

Kath Callaghan, Fiona Balding,
Barbara Monks, Barbara Rathmill
and Suzanne Gray with Louise T. Davies

About this Revision & Practice book

Revise

These pages provide a recap of everything you need to know for each topic.

You should read through all the information before taking the Quick Test at the end. This will test whether you can recall the key facts.

Practise

These topic-based questions appear shortly after the revision pages for each topic and will test whether you have understood the topic. If you get any of the questions wrong, make sure you read the correct answer carefully.

Review

These topic-based questions appear later in the book, allowing you to revisit the topic and test how well you have remembered the information. If you get any of the questions wrong, make sure you read the correct answer carefully.

Mix it Up

These pages feature a mix of questions for all the different topics, just like you would get in an exam. They will make sure you can recall the relevant information to answer a question without being told which topic it relates to.

Test Yourself on the Go

Visit our website at **collins.co.uk/collinsGCSErevision** and print off a set of flashcards. These pocket-sized cards feature questions and answers so that you can test yourself on all the key facts anytime and anywhere. You will also find lots more information about the advantages of spaced practice and how to plan for it.

Workbook

This section features even more topic-based questions as well as practice exam papers, providing two further practice opportunities for each topic to guarantee the best results.

ebook

To access the ebook revision guide visit

collins.co.uk/ebooks

and follow the step-by-step instructions.

QR Codes

Found throughout the book, the QR codes can be scanned on your smartphone for extra practice and explanations.

A QR code in the Revise section links to a Quick Recall Quiz on that topic. A QR code in the Workbook section links to a video working through the solution to one of the questions on that topic.

Contents

Contents

	Revise	Practise	Review

Knife Skills

You must be able to:

- Understand two different methods of using knives to prepare food safely
- Explain the techniques used when preparing different foods that require knife skills.

Knife Holds

Claw Grip

- To use the **claw grip**, shape your hand into a claw shape, tucking the thumb inside the fingers – the knuckle to fingertips part of the hand acts as a barrier against the knife blade when being held in the claw grip shape. It is safer to use a large knife with a flat-sided blade than a smaller one for this reason.
- Place the item you want to cut flat side down on a chopping board and rest the claw on the item to be sliced.
- Hold the knife in the other hand. Use the knife point as a pivot (it should not leave the board). As you slice, the food moves towards the knife; this reduces the health and safety risk.

Bridge Hold

- To use the **bridge hold**, first place the flat surface of the item on a chopping board.
- Now form a bridge with the thumb and index finger of one hand and hold the item on the chopping board.
- Hold a knife in the other hand and position the blade under the bridge formed with your hand. Firmly cut downwards.

Knife Safety Rules

- The correct knife should be used for the appropriate job.
- Knives must be kept sharp and clean; a blunt knife is more likely to cause a cut because more pressure needs to be applied to use it to cut.
- Knife handles must be grease-free.
- The point must always be downwards when carrying a knife.
- Knives should not be put in the washing-up bowl.
- A knife must not be left on the edge of a table or chopping board.

Knife Skills for Vegetable Preparation

- The classic cuts for vegetables are shown in the table.

Claw grip

Bridge hold

> **Key Point**
>
> Specific types of knives are designed for different cutting and shaping tasks.

> **Key Point**
>
> Knives are dangerous if not handled correctly and care should be taken at all times.
>
> A flat and stable cutting surface is essential to avoid injury when cutting food.

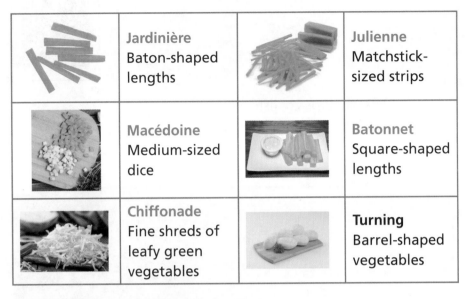

	Jardinière Baton-shaped lengths		**Julienne** Matchstick-sized strips
	Macédoine Medium-sized dice		**Batonnet** Square-shaped lengths
	Chiffonade Fine shreds of leafy green vegetables		**Turning** Barrel-shaped vegetables

Specific Types of Knives

Knife	Description	Uses
Cook's knife	Comes in different sizes. Strong, ridged blade is suitable for a range of tasks.	Dicing, chopping and trimming vegetables, meat, poultry, and fresh herbs.
Paring knife	A small knife with a thin and slightly flexible blade.	Fruit and vegetable preparation.
Boning knife	A very strong blade that will not bend or break easily. May have a straight or curved blade.	Removing bones from meat joints and poultry.
Filleting knife	Thin-bladed, flexible, very sharp knife.	Filleting fish.
Carving knife	Long blade with a serrated or plain edge. Can be rounded or pointed.	Carving meat joints or cooked hams.
Bread knife	Long serrated edge.	Slicing loaves and other bread products.
Palette knife	Flexible blade, which is rounded at the top.	Icing cakes; turning food during cooking; moulding and smoothing food.

Key Words

claw grip	dicing
bridge	chopping
hold	paring
jardinière	flexible
julienne	filleting
macédoine	serrated
chiffonade	cooking
batonnet	

Quick Test

1. How would you carry a knife?
2. Is a blunt knife safer to use than a sharp knife?
3. Why is a flat surface needed to prepare food?
4. Name the two methods of holding food when cutting it.

Quick Recall Quiz

Fish

You must be able to:

- Know how to classify different types of fish
- Explain how to choose, handle and prepare different types of fish.

Classifications of Fish

- There are three main classifications of fish:
  - **White fish** has flesh that is white in colour and contains less fat. White fish can be round or flat, e.g. cod, haddock.
  - **Flat fish** – examples include plaice, sole and halibut.
  - **Oily fish** has flesh that is coloured and contains more fat than white fish but this is healthy fat with fish oils. Examples include salmon, sardines, mackerel and tuna.
- There are two main classifications of **shellfish**:
  - Crustaceans – crabs, lobsters, prawns, crayfish, shrimp and squid (this has a hard backbone that must be removed during preparation).
  - Molluscs – oysters, mussels, scallops, winkles and cockles.

Nutrients Found in Fish

- Nutrients in fish include:
  - Protein – for growth and repair.
  - Minerals – iron, zinc and iodine – for red blood cells, metabolism and to regulate blood sugar.
  - Vitamins A and D – for vision, body linings, the immune system, bone health, and to help with mineral absorption.
- Oily fish contains Omega 3 fatty acids for brain development, healthy bones and joints.

Key Point

White fish carry oil in the liver; oily fish carry oil throughout the flesh.

Buying Quality Fish

- To ensure you are buying quality fish, you need to make sure that: eyes are bright, not dull; scales are in place; gills are bright red; it has a slightly salty, fresh smell of the sea (fish smells bad as it deteriorates); it has a thin layer of slime; the flesh is firm.
- Shellfish must be prepared and eaten within two days of purchase.

Preserving Fish

- There are a number of ways of preserving fish.
- **Canning** – cans are heated to 121 °C to kill bacteria; this heating creates a vacuum inside the can. Any blown or dented cans can cause food poisoning as the vacuum is broken and clostridium botulinum food poisoning can occur.

- **Freezing** – sea fish are frozen within 90 minutes of capture to a minimum temperature of –18 °C. This stops food-poisoning bacteria from reproducing and forces the bacteria to become dormant – it does not kill the bacteria.
- **Smoking** – to 76 °C or above removes moisture from the fish and gives a distinctive flavour, e.g. smoked salmon.
- **Salting** – salt is added to fish to remove its moisture. Food-poisoning bacteria cannot survive without moisture.

Preparing and Cooking Raw Fish

To Prepare	To Cook
<ul><li>Use a blue chopping board (sanitized).</li><li>Use a filleting knife (sharp and sanitized).</li><li>Check for freshness.</li></ul>	<ul><li>Fish cooks quickly because the muscle is short and the **connective tissue** is thin. The connective tissue is made up of collagen and will change into gelatine and **coagulate** at 75 °C.</li><li>Fish can be grilled, baked or fried. Often fish is **enrobed** in breadcrumbs/batter to protect it when using high heat.</li><li>Fish can also be cooked gently by steaming or poaching without coating the flesh.</li></ul>

Key Point

It's important to wash your hands after handling fish to prevent cross-contamination.

Filleting a Flat Fish

	Use a filleting knife to descale and remove the fins. Cut off the head just behind the gills.
	Cut from head to tail down to the bone, to one side of the centre line.
	Turn the knife almost parallel to the table. Make a long, smooth cut. Cut horizontally against the backbone towards the outer edge. Separate the fillet from the bone and remove it.

Filleting a Round Fish

	Descale and remove the fins. Cut into the top of the fish on one side of the tail; detach the backbone from head to tail.
	Cut under the flesh towards the tail and detach the cut piece.
	Cut along the curved rib bones and finish detaching the fillet at the head. Turn the fish over and repeat to remove the second fillet.

Quick Test

1. Which type of fish contains the most Omega 3 fatty acids?
2. Describe **two** quality checks for fresh fish.
3. What equipment is needed when preparing raw fish?

Key Words

crustacean
mollusc
smoking
salting
connective
tissue
coagulate
enrobed

Meat

You must be able to:

- Know the main sources of meat and how they are prepared
- Understand the structure of meat and how this affects the cooking method used.

Nutritional Content

- Meat contains:
  - Protein, including **collagen**, **elastin** and **myoglobin**, which makes the meat red in colour.
  - Fat (saturated) – provides warmth and protection of the animal's internal organs.
  - Minerals, e.g. iron, calcium and phosphorus – needed to form red blood cells, bones and teeth, and for energy metabolism.
  - Vitamins B6 and B12 – needed to release energy from foods.
  - Cholesterol.

> **Key Point**
>
> The length and type of cooking method depends on the type of **muscle fibre**.

Classifications of Meat

- Meat is classified as the muscle tissue of dead animals and birds.
- There are four main meat sources:
  - Animals: pork (pigs), beef (cattle), lamb (sheep).
  - Poultry: chicken, turkey, duck, goose.
  - Game: feathered or furred; venison, rabbit, pheasant.
  - Offal: liver, tongue, tripe, kidney, heart, brain, trotters.

The Structure of Meat

- Meat is a muscle made of cells, which consist of fibres held together by connective tissue. Long fibres are associated with tough meat – the older an animal is, the tougher the meat.
- Muscles that work a lot, such as the thighs and shoulders of animals, give tough meat, e.g. shin beef, brisket. Small fibres are associated with tender cuts.

Meat Cuts and Cooking

- Cuts of meat from muscle areas that do a lot of work will need longer, slower cooking methods in wet heat, e.g. stewing, braising, pot roasting and casseroling.
- Meat from tougher cuts can be ground or minced to break up the connective tissues so that it cooks more quickly.
- Cuts of meat from muscle areas not so heavily used by the animal, e.g. the back and the rump, can be cooked much more quickly in dry heat, e.g. grilling, stir-frying.

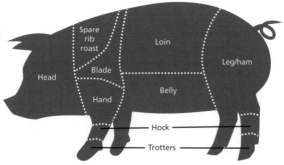

Marinating and Tenderising

- Marinades are added to meat before cooking to add flavour and the acid content of the marinade (e.g. lemon juice, yoghurt, wine) breaks down the protein in the meat.
- Meat is tenderised by: using a marinade; mincing; or using a steak hammer.

The Effects of Cooking Meat

- The browning of meat is caused by a reaction with natural sugars and proteins to produce a dark colour. This is called the Maillard reaction or non-enzymic browning.
- As meat cooks, the proteins coagulate due to heat. Collagen breaks down into gelatine, making the meat tender.

Checking for Readiness

- You should know the safety rules for cooking different meat.
- Meat joints can be tested using a meat probe or temperature probe. To determine if a steak is rare, medium or well done the 'poke' test can be learned and used.
- The following foods should not be eaten if undercooked: chicken (80 °C), pork (75 °C), offal and game, burgers, sausages, kebabs.

Cooking Different Meat Joints

Meat	Temperature	Time per 500 g
Pork	75–80 °C	30 mins + 15 mins
Poultry	75–80 °C	20 mins + 20 mins
Beef	Rare: 52 °C	20 mins
Lamb	Medium: 62°C	25 mins
	Well done: 75–80 °C	30 mins

Boning a Chicken

- Do not wash the chicken. Place **whole chicken** on a red board.
- Remove the legs. Cut down through the skin and between the joints. Turn the chicken over and break the legs.
- Find the knuckle and cut through the leg to separate the **drumstick** and the **thigh**.
- Cut through the joints to remove the **wings**.
- Find the wishbone at the front of the bird. Cut a V-shape on either side of the bird to release the wishbone, then cut through the knuckle at the base. Carefully remove the **breasts** from the carcass.

Storing Meat Safely

- Raw meat should be kept separate from cooked meat to avoid cross-contamination.
- Raw meat should be stored covered at the bottom of the fridge so meat juices cannot drip onto other foods.
- Cooked meat should be kept chilled and covered and treated as a high-risk food.
- Chilled meat should be stored at between 1 °C and 4 °C.
- Frozen meat should be stored at between −18 °C and −22 °C.

Quick Test

1. Where would you store meat when not preparing it?
2. Tough meat has what length of fibres?
3. What are the main sources of meat?

Key Words

collagen
elastin
myoglobin
muscle fibre
Maillard reaction
non-enzymic browning
gelatine
cross-contamination

Prepare, Combine and Shape

Quick Recall Quiz

You must be able to:

- Understand that a recipe consists of specific quantities of ingredients that are prepared, using a variety of skills, to produce the required outcome
- Know that ingredients can be combined and shaped to make the finished dish more attractive and appetising to the consumer.

Methods for Cutting and Preparing Ingredients

- **Slicing:** slicing even-sized cuts to suit the requirements of the dish.
- **Peeling:** using a peeler or knife to remove skin from fruit or vegetables, although it can be beneficial to leave skin on as it contains Non-Starch Polysaccharides (NSP) or fibre.
- **Chopping:** cutting ingredients into small pieces, precise sizes or roughly chopped.
- **Dicing:** cutting into cubes.
- **Grating:** passing food over a blade to reduce food in order to achieve the required size or thickness.
- **Coring:** removing the centre core of vegetables and fruit.
- **Mashing/crushing**: pressing into a puree or crushing into small pieces perhaps with the skin left on for added fibre.
- **Shredding:** grating or slicing into thin long flexible strips.
- **Scissor snipping:** using scissors to cut to the required shape, size or length.
- **Scooping:** using a spoon, scoop or melon baller to remove small circular pieces from the ingredient.
- **Segmenting:** cutting even-sized pieces from the ingredient, removing pith, zest and membrane.
- **Skinning:** peeling, grating, zesting or slicing off the outer skin from the ingredient.
- **Blanching:** placing the ingredient into boiling water for a few minutes to quickly cook, soften and inhibit the enzymic activity.
- **Blending:** using an electric food processor or blender to process different food ingredients together to form one product or sauce.
- **Juicing:** squeezing an ingredient to remove the liquid from it.
- **Preparing garnishes** – for example, zesting, carving, making ribbons, crisps, twists, roses, and using edible flowers.

Peeling food

Grating food

> ### Key Point
>
> Enzymic activity occurs when cut fruit and vegetables react with oxygen to turn them brown.

Combining and Shaping Ingredients

- Ingredients can be combined or mixed in a number of ways:
  - Whisking – combining ingredients to incorporate air into a mixture, e.g. meringues.
  - Stirring – gently mixing ingredients with a spoon.
  - Folding – gently incorporating mixtures together, such as flour into a cake mixture.

Stirring food (Stirfry)

- Creaming – mixing two ingredients together, such as sugar and butter in cake making.
- **Rubbing-in** – incorporating fat into flour when making pastry.
- Ingredients can be shaped in a number of ways:
  - By hand – to achieve an even shape, for example, when making fishcakes, meatballs, falafels and koftas.
  - In a mould – e.g. to form the shape of bread loaves, mousses.
  - Using cutters – dough can be cut precisely to keep consistency.
  - With a rolling pin – used to achieve a desired thickness.
  - Using a piping bag – shaped nozzles create patterns, e.g. duchess potato.

Binding, Coating and Glazing

Binding

- **Binding** means holding ingredients together.
- Egg acts as a binding agent to hold ingredients together in burgers.
- Water binds flour and fat in pastry to help form a dough; some enriched shortcrust pastries use egg yolk to bind.
- Potato and/or flour are used as a binding material in fish cakes.
- Breadcrumbs are used as a binder in sausage mixtures.

Coating

- **Coating** means adding an outer layer to a food.
- Breadcrumbs are used for coating fish cakes and chicken **goujons**.
- Batters are used to enrobe, coat and protect fish and fritters that are deep-fried.
- Chocolate can be used as a coating to hold food together.

Glazing

- Egg wash **glaze** has a golden, shiny finish and is good for pastry and dough.
- Egg white has a crisp, golden texture and is good for sweet pastry dishes.
- Egg yolk gives a golden brown colour and works well on potato dishes.
- Milk gives a golden brown glaze for scones, pastry and biscuits.
- Sugar and water form a sweet, sticky covering used on **enriched dough**.
- Jam gives a shiny finish and is brushed over fruit flans.
- Arrowroot is a clear shiny gel that is used to finish fruit flans.

 Key Point

Various foods can be coated with ingredients to create a new layer to protect, add texture and flavour – this is called coating, or enrobing.

 Key Words

ingredients
precise
combined
rubbing-in
binding
coating
goujons
enriched dough

Quick Test

1. How would you shape meatballs?
2. What would you use to shape a burger?
3. What glaze would you use on enriched dough?

Dough

Quick Recall Quiz

You must be able to:

- Know that making and shaping dough is a precursor to making a variety of flour-based mixtures
- Understand the function of ingredients in dough.

Bread Dough

- Bread dough is made with a strong plain flour, which contains a high level (17%) of the proteins gliadin and glutenin.
- Gluten is produced when water is added to the flour, enabling strong elastic dough to be formed.
- The elasticity of the dough helps to trap carbon dioxide gas (CO_2), which is produced by the yeast to raise the dough.

The Function of Ingredients in Bread

- Each ingredient in bread has a specific function:
  - A **strong flour** is used as it has a high gluten content.
  - **Yeast** is the raising agent, producing carbon dioxide.
  - **Warm liquid** is needed to form the dough and encourage the yeast to grow.
  - **Salt** adds flavour, and aids gluten development.
  - **Fat** extends the shelf-life and adds colour and flavour.

> **Key Point**
>
> Dough is made by mixing flour with liquid, and sometimes includes leavening (raising) agents as well as other ingredients and flavourings.

Enriched Dough

- **Enriched dough** is a basic bread dough with the addition of sugar, butter and sometimes egg.
- Additional flavourings such as mixed spices, dried fruit and nuts can be added.
- Examples of enriched dough include teacakes, panettone and stollen.

Pastries

- Different types of pastry are used for sweet or savoury dishes. They include:
  - shortcrust
  - choux
  - flaky/rough puff
  - suet
  - hot-water crust
  - filo pastry
  - puff pastry.

Shortcrust Pastry

- Shortcrust pastry uses the rubbing-in method and is used for making pies and tarts.
- The **ratio** of ingredients is half fat to flour (1:2).
- Soft (plain) flour is used as it contains less gluten.
- Fats – a mixture of 50% lard (shortness) and 50% butter/margarine (colour and flavour) creates ideal shortening.
- Water binds the mixture. Salt adds flavour and aids the chemical reaction.
- Fat coats the flour and restricts the amount of gluten formed.
- The texture should be short, crisp and light.

Choux Pastry

- Choux pastry is used for eclairs, choux buns and gougères.
- All the ingredients must be weighed accurately.
- Strong flour is used to form the structure of the choux.
- Water and fat is brought to a **rolling boil** and the flour is added in one go immediately then mixed vigorously until the paste forms a soft ball (roux). The paste is cooled; beaten eggs are then added gradually to a **heavy dropping consistency**.
- The pastry is cooked in a hot oven.
- When the choux is baked, the water turns to steam and raises the dough and the egg protein coagulates to set the structure.

Pasta

- Pasta is made from strong wheat flour called Durum wheat, which has a high gluten content and is usually labelled type '00'.
- The liquid can be olive oil or egg. Ingredients such as spinach, tomato puree, squid ink or beetroot add colour.
- The flour and liquid are mixed then kneaded to develop the gluten content; then the dough is **rested**.
- The dough is rolled using a machine or by hand until thin and air dried. It can be made into a variety of shapes and filled.

 Key Point

The way dough is handled during preparation affects the outcome.

 Key Words

gliadin
glutenin
gluten
carbon dioxide gas (CO_2)
shortcrust
choux
ratio
rolling boil
heavy dropping
  consistency
rest

> **Quick Test**
>
> 1. What type of flour is used to make bread dough?
> 2. What gas does yeast produce?
> 3. What is the function of fat in shortcrust pastry?

Practice Questions

Knife Skills

1 What **two** joints would you get from a chicken leg? Tick (✓) **two** answers. [2]

a) Breast ☐   b) Wing ☐

c) Drumstick ☐   d) Thigh ☐

2 Name and describe **two** vegetable knife cuts. [4]

Example: brunoise	Very small dice

3 Name three vegetable cuts that require you to cut the ingredient into vertical strips. [3]

Fish

1 Which of the following fish would you expect to find preserved in a can? Tick (✓) one answer. [1]

a) Cod ☐   b) Plaice ☐

c) Sardine ☐   d) Halibut ☐

2 Which choice would **not** be suitable when enrobing a fish fillet before cooking?
Tick (✓) one answer. [1]

a) Breadcrumbs ☐   b) Polenta ☐

c) Batter ☐   d) Chocolate ☐

3 Give **one** example of each of the following classifications of fish:

a) White fish _____ [1]

b) Flat fish _____ [1]

c) Oily fish _____ [1]

4 Explain how you would select a quality fish when buying from a fresh fish counter. [5]

_____

_____

_____

_____

_____

_____

_____

_____

Meat

1 Which term best describes the structure of meat? Tick (✓) one answer. [1]

a) Meat is the flesh of animals. ☐

b) Meat is muscle composed of fibres held together by connective tissue. ☐

c) Meat is a combination of flesh and fat held together by connective tissue. ☐

d) Meat is a combination of tender and tough muscle fibres. ☐

2 Which of these statements is **not** true? Tick (✓) one answer. [1]

a) Tender meat comes from younger animals. ☐

b) Tender meat has shorter muscle fibres. ☐

c) Tougher meat cuts can be minced to break up connective tissue. ☐

d) Tougher meat comes from parts of the animal that do the least work. ☐

3 This question is about cooking meat. Name **two** methods suitable for cooking each of the following types of meat:

a) Shin beef _____ [2]

b) Rump steak _____ [2]

c) Hamburger _____ [2]

4️⃣ Complete the following table for cooking meat joints. [4]

Meat	Temperature Check	Time per 500 g
Pork	75 °C or above (in England) 82 °C or above (in Scotland)	.... mins + 15 mins
Poultry	75–82 °C or above	20 mins + ... mins
Beef and Lamb	Rare: 52 °C Medium: .... °C .... : 75–80 °C	20 mins 25 mins 30 mins

5️⃣ Name **two** meats that must be cooked fully to be safe to eat. [2]

Prepare, Combine and Shape

1️⃣ Which glaze would be most suitable for a batch of Chelsea buns? Tick (✓) one answer. [1]

a) Egg wash ☐   b) Arrowroot ☐

c) Sugar and water ☐   d) Egg yolk ☐

2️⃣ Name **two** foods from the choices below that would best demonstrate each of the food preparation methods listed in the table. [8]

apple	cheese	carrot	onion

bread	pineapple	herbs

Method	Food
Grating	
Chopping	
Slicing	
De-coring	

Dough

1   What is the most suitable flour for making **choux pastry**? Tick (✓) one answer.   [1]

   a) Plain flour ☐   **b)** Strong plain flour ☐

   c) Self-raising flour ☐   **d)** Cornflour ☐

2   What is the ratio of fat to flour in shortcrust pastry? Tick (✓) one answer.   [1]

   a) 1:1 ☐   **b)** 1:2 ☐

   c) 1:3 ☐   **d)** 1:4 ☐

3   What type of wheat is used to make pasta? _____   [1]

4   What are the names of the proteins found in a strong flour?   [2]

_____   _____

5   Name **two** foods that can be added to pasta dough to give colour.   [2]

_____ and _____

6   How can you make sure that pasta dough will roll out easily in a pasta machine?   [2]

_____

7   Complete the following instructions for making quality choux dough. Use the key word(s) to start each instruction off.

   a) Weigh _____   [1]

   b) Add flour _____   [1]

   c) Add eggs _____   [1]

   d) Consistency _____   [1]

   e) Bake _____   [1]

Protein and Fat

Quick Recall Quiz

You must be able to:

- Demonstrate knowledge and understanding of the functions, structures and main sources of protein and fat
- Know the biological value of protein
- Understand the consequences of excess and deficiencies of both protein and fat.

Protein

- Protein is a macronutrient.
- Protein is formed from chains of simpler units called amino acids.
- Eight amino acids need to be provided by the diet and are called essential amino acids. Children require two additional amino acids.
- Protein is used for specific functions in the body: growth, repair, maintenance, and as a secondary energy source.

Sources of Protein

- Animal sources – meat, fish, poultry, milk, eggs, cheese, insects.
- Plant sources – soya, nuts, seeds, pulses (e.g. lentils), mycoprotein (Quorn), TVP (Texturised Vegetable Protein).

The Biological Value of Proteins

- The biological value of protein means the amount of essential amino acids present.
- Animal protein sources contain all the essential amino acids required by the body; they are of High Biological Value (HBV).
- Mycoprotein (Quorn) and Texturised Vegetable Protein (TVP) are of HBV too.
- Proteins from plant sources are of Low Biological Value (LBV) and lack some essential amino acids. The exception is soya, which is a plant protein of HBV.

Protein Complementation

- Proteins of LBV can be eaten together to provide all the essential amino acids, for example, beans on toast. This is protein complementation.
- Protein complementation is important for vegetarians and vegans.

Protein Excess and Deficiencies

- Excess protein in the diet is used as energy.
- Protein deficiencies are rare but in developing countries kwashiorkor is a severe form of protein malnutrition.
- Some groups of people have a higher need for protein. They are:
  - babies and children – for growth
  - adolescents – for growth spurts
  - pregnant women – for the growing baby
  - nursing mothers – for lactation (milk production).

> ### Key Point
>
> Protein is required by the body for growth, maintenance and repair. Proteins are built up of units of amino acids.

Fat

- Fat is a macronutrient. It can be solid or liquid.
- Fat is made up of **fatty acids** and **glycerol**.
- Fatty acids can be described as **saturated fats** or **unsaturated fats**.
- The structure of fatty acids influences their effect on our health.
- The characteristics of fatty acids influence cooking choice.

Functions of Fat in the Diet

- Fat provides concentrated energy.
- Fat is a source of **fat-soluble vitamins** A, D, E and K.
- Fat provides protection for the major organs in the body.
- Fat is a component of hormones.

Sources of Fat in the Diet

- Saturated fats:
  - Saturated fats can increase the **cholesterol** level in the blood.
  - Too much cholesterol can lead to health problems.
  - Sources of cholesterol include butter, ghee, lard, cream, hard cheese, meat pies, coconut oil and palm oil.
- Unsaturated fats:
  - Unsaturated fats can help reduce cholesterol in the blood.
  - Sources include: oily fish, nuts, seeds, avocados, vegetable oils, soya beans, and some functional foods, such as cholesterol-lowering spreads.

Hydrogenated Fat and Trans Fats

- Making solid fat from a liquid oil is called **hydrogenation**.
- **Trans fats** can be formed when oil goes through the process of hydrogenation to form a solid. This process occurs as the molecules flip and rotate.

Fat Excess and Deficiencies

- Fat is only needed in small amounts and excess fat in the diet can lead to weight gain, obesity and related medical conditions.
- Excess saturated fat raises blood cholesterol levels.
- Trans fats have been linked to health problems including heart disease and some cancers.
- Fat deficiency in babies and children could affect normal growth.
- Fat deficiency could result in a poor supply of fat-soluble vitamins.

Key Point

Fats can be classified as either saturated and unsaturated. Saturated fats are considered to be more harmful to health because they raise levels of cholesterol.

Key Words

amino acids
essential amino acids
High Biological Value (HBV)
Low Biological Value (LBV)
protein complementation
kwashiorkor
fatty acids
glycerol
saturated fats
unsaturated fats
fat-soluble vitamins
cholesterol
hydrogenation
trans fats

Quick Test

1. What are the functions of fat in the diet?
2. What are the simple units of protein called?
3. Give an example of protein complementation.

Carbohydrate

Quick Recall Quiz

You must be able to:

- Know and understand the functions, structures and main sources of carbohydrate
- Understand an individual's need for carbohydrate
- Demonstrate a knowledge and understanding of the consequences of consumption of excess carbohydrate and of deficiencies in carbohydrate.

Carbohydrate

- The body's cells require a constant supply of carbohydrate, which is used as fuel to provide energy.
- Sugars and starches are types of carbohydrate.
- **Dietary fibre** is also a type of carbohydrate but it cannot be digested to provide energy.
- Carbohydrates are produced mainly by plants during the process of photosynthesis.
- Carbohydrates can be classified according to their structure: monosaccharides, disaccharides, polysaccharides.

> **Key Point**
>
> Carbohydrate provides the body with energy. Most of our energy should come from starchy foods.

Monosaccharides	Disaccharides	Polysaccharides
Monosaccharides are the simplest form of carbohydrate structure. They include: – Glucose – all other carbohydrate is converted into this in the body. – Galactose – found in the milk of mammals. – Fructose – found in fruit.	Disaccharides are more complex sugars that are formed when two monosaccharides join together. They include: – Sucrose – Maltose – Lactose	Polysaccharides are made up of many monosaccharides units joined together. They include: – Starch – many glucose units formed together. – Glycogen – formed after digestion. – Dietary fibre. – Dextrin – toasted crust on bread; sugars caramelise on the surface. – Cellulose – formed by plants from glucose. – Pectin – found in fruit, forms a gel on cooking.

Function and Sources of Carbohydrate

- Sugars are digested quickly in the body, providing instant energy.
- Sugars are found in a variety of sources including table sugar (sucrose), honey and jam, fruit juice, sweets and chocolate, fruit and vegetables.
- Eating starchy foods rather than sugary foods is the healthier way to provide the body with energy. Starch (a polysaccharide) is found in bread, pasta, rice, breakfast cereals and potatoes.
- Starches have to be digested into sugars before absorption – this is slow energy release.

Excess and Deficiencies of Carbohydrate

- Excess carbohydrate is converted to fat and is stored under the skin; this is the main cause of obesity.
- Excess sugar in the diet is linked to dental decay.
- There is evidence to suggest that the rise in Type 2 diabetes is linked to diets high in sugar.
- If insufficient carbohydrate is eaten, the body will firstly start to use protein and fat as an energy source.

Dietary Fibre

- The scientific name for fibre is Non–Starch Polysaccharide (NSP).
- Soluble NSP absorbs water, forming a gel-like substance. This can inhibit the absorption of cholesterol.
- Insoluble NSP is not absorbed by the body. It passes through the body as waste, which helps prevent bowel diseases.

Function and Sources of Dietary Fibre

- Dietary fibre absorbs water in the intestine and enables waste food (faeces) to be expelled from the body quickly and easily.
- Dietary fibre can be found in wholemeal bread, wholegrain breakfast cereals (e.g. bran flakes, shredded wheat, porridge oats) wholemeal pasta and wholemeal flour; fruit and vegetables; potato skins; dried fruit, nuts and seeds, beans, peas and lentils.
- Adults should consume at least 18 g of fibre per day.
- Young children must gradually add high fibre foods to their diets.
- Fibre deficiency can lead to:
  - **Constipation** – this is when faeces become difficult to expel from the body because they are hard and small.
  - **Diverticular disease** – pouches form in the intestines, which become infected with bacteria.
- A low-fibre diet can be linked to cancer, particularly bowel cancer.

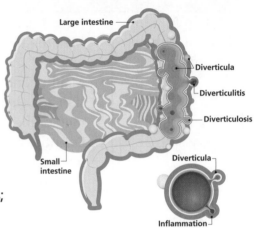

Labels: Large intestine, Diverticula, Diverticulitis, Diverticulosis, Small intestine, Diverticula, Inflammation

Quick Test

1. What is the function of carbohydrate in the body?
2. What happens if too much carbohydrate is eaten?
3. What does NSP stand for?

Key Words

dietary fibre
photosynthesis
monosaccharides
disaccharides
polysaccharides
Non–Starch
 Polysaccharide (NSP)
constipation
diverticular disease

Vitamins

You must be able to:

- Demonstrate knowledge and understanding of the sources and functions of both fat-soluble and water-soluble vitamins
- Know and understand the consequences of excess and deficiencies of fat-soluble and water-soluble vitamins
- Understand the retention of water-soluble vitamins during cooking.

Fat-soluble Vitamins

Vitamin	Function in the Body	Sources	Deficiency/Excess
Vitamin A (Retinol, Beta carotene)	• Normal iron metabolism • Maintenance of normal vision • Maintenance of skin and the mucus membranes • Essential for maintaining healthy immune function.	• Animal sources – liver and whole milk (retinol) • Plant sources – green leafy vegetables, carrots, and orange-coloured fruits (carotenoids) • Margarine, which is fortified by law	• Excess can be toxic, causing liver and bone damage • Excess retinol can lead to birth defects • Deficiency can cause night blindness
Vitamin D (Cholecalciferol)	• Absorption and use of calcium and phosphorus • Maintenance and strength of bones and teeth	• Dietary sources – oily fish, meat, eggs and fortified breakfast cereals and margarines (vitamin D added by law) • Sunlight on the skin	Deficiencies: • Bones that become weak and bend • Rickets in children • Osteomalacia in adults • Weak teeth
Vitamin E (Tocopherol)	• Antioxidant that helps protect cell membranes • Maintains healthy skin and eyes	• Polyunsaturated fats, e.g. sunflower oils • Nuts, seeds and wheatgerm	• A deficiency is very rare
Vitamin K (Phytomenadione)	• Normal clotting of blood	• Green leafy vegetables, cheese, bacon and liver	• A deficiency is rare • Newborn babies are given a dose of vitamin K

Water-soluble Vitamins

Vitamin	Function in the Body	Sources	Deficiency
Vitamin B1 (thiamin)	• Release of energy from carbohydrates • Nervous system function • Normal growth of children	• Wholegrain products • Meat • Milk and dairy • Nuts • Marmite • Fortified breakfast cereals • Fortified white and brown flour	• Beri-beri, which affects the nervous system

Vitamin B2 (riboflavin)	• Energy release from foods • Healthy nervous system	• Same as vitamin B1 thiamin	• Cracking skin around the mouth • Swollen tongue • Failure to grow
Folate (Folic acid)	• Neural tube development in unborn babies	• Green leafy vegetables • Potatoes, asparagus, bananas • Beans, seeds and nuts • Wholegrain products • Breakfast cereals	• Spina bifida in unborn babies. Pre conception and pregnant women need a good supply
Vitamin B12 (cobalamin)	• Supports production of energy • Protective coating around nerve cells	• Meat and fish • Cheese, eggs and milk • Marmite • Fortified breakfast cereals	• Pernicious anaemia
Vitamin C – (ascorbic acid)	• Absorption of iron • Production of collagen that binds connective tissue • Vitamin C is an antioxidant which helps protect the body from pollutants	• Citrus fruits • Kiwi fruit • Blackcurrants • Potatoes • Tomatoes and green vegetables, e.g. broccoli, kale	• Weak connective tissue and blood vessels • Bleeding gums and loose teeth • Anaemia • Severe cases – scurvy

Vitamins and Food Preparation

- Vitamins B and C are water-soluble so will dissolve into water during cooking. Vitamin C is destroyed on exposure to oxygen.
- To maximise vitamin retention:
  - prepare foods quickly just before serving
  - use small amounts of boiling water to cook
  - use cooking liquid to make sauces
  - avoid lots of cutting of vegetables
  - water soluble vitamins – avoid cooking in water, instead steam, roast, fry or grill
  - fat-soluble vitamins – avoid cooking in fat, instead boil, steam or grill.
- Vitamins A, C and E contain antioxidants which work together to protect cell membranes.

Key Point

Vitamins are micronutrients, required in small amounts to do essential jobs in the body.

Key Point

Water-soluble vitamins are easily destroyed during preparation and cooking.

Key Words

fortified
rickets
osteomalacia
antioxidant
thiamin
riboflavin
spina bifida
cobalamin
ascorbic acid

Quick Test

1. What are the fat-soluble vitamins?
2. Give **three** good sources of vitamin C.
3. Which vitamin is connected with the healthy development of the spine in unborn babies?

Minerals and Water

You must be able to:

- Demonstrate knowledge and understanding of the functions and main sources of calcium, iron, sodium, iodine and fluoride
- Show knowledge and understanding of the consequences of deficiencies of calcium, iron, sodium, iodine and fluoride in the diet
- Know and understand the function of water in the diet.

Minerals

- Minerals are micronutrients.
- Minerals include calcium, iron, fluoride, sodium and iodine.

> **Key Point**
>
> Minerals are required in small amounts and have a variety of essential functions in the body.

Calcium

Function	Sources	Deficiency
• Strengthens bones and teeth – with Vitamin D • Bones are able to reach peak bone mass – maximum strength • Growth of children • Clots blood after injury • Promotes nerves and muscles to work properly.	• Milk and dairy foods • Green leafy vegetables • White bread – calcium is added by law • Soya products • Fish eaten with the bones, e.g. sardines 	• Bones don't reach peak bone mass and become weak and break easily – common in older people (osteoporosis). • During pregnancy, a woman's teeth and bones weaken. • Poor clotting of the blood.

Iron

Function	Sources	Deficiency
• Supports the production of haemoglobin in red blood cells; this transports oxygen around the body • Vitamin C is required to absorb iron.	• Red meat – liver • Lentils, dried apricots, cocoa, chocolate, corned beef and curry spices • Green leafy vegetables, e.g. spinach • Breakfast cereals fortified with iron.	• Iron deficiency is called anaemia; symptoms include tiredness • Anaemia is a common condition in teenage girls and women due to blood loss in menstruation. • Pregnant women may become deficient due to additional blood needed to support the growing baby.

Fluoride

Function	Sources	Deficiency
• To strengthen the enamel layer of teeth.	• Saltwater fish, tea • Some water authorities fortify their water supply with fluoride.	• Teeth may develop cavities and require filling.

Sodium

Function	Sources	Excess and Deficiency
• Needed by the body to regulate the amount of water in the body • Needed to assist the body in the use of energy • Required to help control muscles and nerves.	• Processed foods – for flavour and as a preservative • Salt added to food in home cooking for flavour • Salt added at the table.	• A deficiency is rare, but can lead to muscle cramps after exercise in hot conditions • People suffering with sickness and diarrhoea can lose salt • Excess salt in the diet is linked to high blood pressure, heart disease and strokes.

Iodine

Function	Sources	Deficiency
• Regulates hormones in the thyroid, which controls the body's metabolic rate.	• Seafood • Foods grown in iodine-rich soils.	• Poor functioning of the thyroid gland, resulting in feeling tired and lethargic • A goitre (swelling) in the thyroid gland.

Water

- The body is nearly two-thirds water. The functions of water are:
  - For normal brain function
  - To decrease risk of kidney problems
  - For normal blood pressure
  - To help bowel movements
  - To regulate temperature and maintain hydration
  - To make body fluids – blood, saliva, mucus membranes.
- The main sources of water are drinking water, milk, tea, coffee and fruit juices.
- The remaining 20% of water needed comes from foods such as soup, yoghurt, fruit and vegetables.
- Water should be drunk every day. 6–8 glasses daily is recommended.
- People with increased water needs are:
  - Those with an active lifestyle during hot weather – water needs increase due to perspiration.
  - Anyone suffering vomiting or diarrhoea, to avoid dehydration.
  - Lactating mothers (breast feeding), for milk production.
  - Elderly people, to help prevent kidney problems and infections.
  - During hot weather water needs increase due to perspiration.

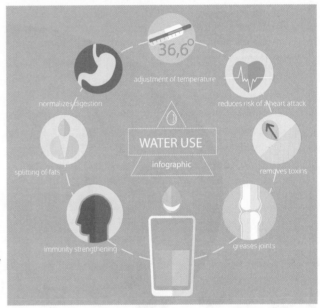

Key Point

Water makes up two thirds of the body so it is vital to drink regularly to stay hydrated.

Key Words

peak bone mass
haemoglobin
anaemia
thyroid
dehydration
lactating

Quick Test

1. Why do teenage girls need an increased supply of iron?
2. What is peak bone mass?
3. Which hormones in the body are affected by a lack of iodine?
4. Name **two** good sources of calcium in the diet.

Making Informed Choices

You must be able to:

- Demonstrate knowledge and understanding of the Eatwell Guide and the Healthy Eating Guidelines
- Have knowledge and understanding of the diet requirements throughout life.

The Eatwell Guide

- The **Eatwell Guide** shows the proportions of food groups that should be eaten daily in a well-balanced diet.

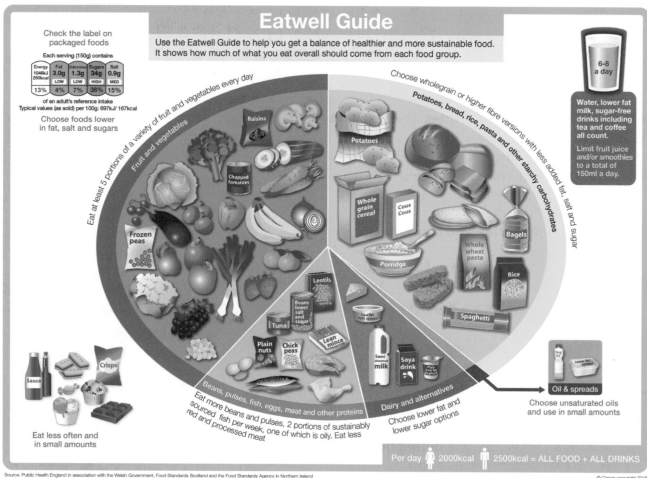

Guidelines for a Healthy Diet

- Base your meals on starchy carbohydrates.
- Eat lots of fruit and vegetables (5–7 portions per day).
- Eat plenty of fish, including oily fish.
- Cut down on saturated fat and sugars.
- Eat less salt – no more than 6g a day for adults.
- Get active and be a healthy weight.
- Don't get thirsty (drink 6–8 of water a day).
- Don't skip breakfast.

> **Key Point**
>
> Nutritional needs change throughout life, but everyone needs to consider the current healthy eating guidelines when planning meals.

Nutritional Needs Throughout Life

Babies:

- Newborn babies should have only milk for the first 4–6 months of life.
- First milk is called colostrum and it is full of antibodies.
- Human milk provides babies with all their nutritional requirements, except for iron. Babies are born with a supply of iron stored in the liver.
- The introduction of solid foods is called 'weaning'.

Children

- Toddlers aged 1–3 years grow rapidly and so it is essential they get a well-balanced diet to support their physical development.
- Toddlers are physically very active and need a good supply of fat, which also helps the development of the brain and nervous system.
- New healthy foods need to be introduced in an attractive and appealing way.
- Sweets, biscuits, cakes and fizzy drinks must be avoided. Sugary foods cause dental decay and are strongly linked to obesity.

Teenagers

- Adolescence is a period of rapid growth and this is when puberty occurs.
- The need for energy and most nutrients is relatively high.
- After menstruation begins, girls need more iron to replace blood losses. Iron-deficiency anaemia is common in teenage girls.

Pregnancy

- A healthy diet is required in pregnancy to ensure the baby receives the essential nutrients required for development.
- Folate (Folic acid) is needed both before and during early pregnancy for the development of the neural tube of the foetus.
- The baby's bones require a good supply of calcium from the mother's diet.
- A pregnant mother will need a diet rich in iron for the production of additional blood supply and to lay down an iron store in the baby's liver.
- Constipation is common in pregnancy so a diet high in dietary fibre (NSP) is important.

Older people

- In older people energy requirements decrease. They will require smaller portions at meal times.
- Older people need to keep hydrated by drinking plenty of fluids.
- Osteoporosis may occur when bones become weak, brittle and break easily.
- Older people are advised to eat calcium-rich foods to help strengthen bones.

 Quick Test

1. Give **three** recommended guidelines to a healthy diet.
2. Why is a good supply of folate (folic acid) needed in early pregnancy?
3. What is colostrum?
4. In babies, what is the introduction of solid foods called?
5. What is osteoporosis?

Key Words

Eatwell Guide
colostrum
puberty
menstruation
iron-deficiency anaemia
foetus
osteoporosis

Diet, Nutrition and Health

You must be able to:

- Demonstrate knowledge and understanding of the health conditions linked to food and nutrition
- Demonstrate knowledge and understanding of the terms relating to diet, health and energy needs.

Quick Recall Quiz

Diet-related Medical Conditions

Obesity, Coronary Heart Disease and Type 2 Diabetes

- **Obesity** is an abnormal accumulation of body fat. Obesity is associated with coronary heart disease, diabetes, some cancers and high blood pressure.
- **Coronary heart disease** is caused by fatty substances (cholesterol) building up in the walls of the arteries that run to the heart.
- Arteries narrow, reducing the supply of oxygen to the heart.
- Diets high in saturated fats produce cholesterol. Most people should reduce their intake of saturated fat.
- **High blood pressure** can lead to an increased risk of stroke and can be linked to increased salt intake. The recommended amount of salt to be consumed per day is 6 grams. Many people consume too much salt, which is often hidden in processed foods.
- With **Type 2 diabetes** either too little insulin is produced, or the body's cells fail to react to the insulin that is produced. This results in high levels of sugar in the blood.
- Diabetes is controlled by careful management of sugar in the diet, plus insulin medication frequently injected.
- Type 2 diabetes is increasingly linked to obesity and high sugar consumption.

> **Key Point**
>
> Obesity is the main cause of diet-related illness in the UK.

Iron Deficiency Anaemia

- Anaemia is common in teenage girls due to menstruation.
- Symptoms of anaemia include tiredness, lack of energy, shortness of breath and pale complexion.
- Pregnant women also need increased iron supplies in the diet.
- Anaemia is simply diagnosed with a blood test.

Dental Health and Bone Health

- Sugar is a major cause of **tooth decay** in children.
- Sugar increases acids on the teeth, causing irreparable damage.
- In tooth decay, acids erode the protective white enamel surface of the teeth.
- **Osteoporosis** is common in old age. Bones can become weak, brittle and more likely to break. It also causes the spine to curve forward, making walking difficult.
- A diet rich in calcium and vitamin D is required to ensure maximum bone strength.

> **Key Point**
>
> Osteoporosis means 'porous bones' – the bones lose their strength and are more likely to break.

Bowel Cancer
- Bowel cancer is the second biggest illness/cause of death in the UK.
- The risk of bowel cancer and diverticular disease can be greatly reduced by increasing fibre/NSP (non-starch polysaccharide) intake.

Energy Needs

- Energy is required for us to grow, to keep the basic functions of our body going, and to be physically active.
- Energy requirements depend on your Basal Metabolic Rate (BMR). BMR is the energy needed by the body to power your internal organs when completely at rest.
- An individual's BMR depends on their age, gender and body size.
- We use energy for movement of all types, known as Physical Activity Level (PAL). More physically active people require more food to supply their energy needs.
- Nutritionists devise Estimated Average Requirements (EARs) tables that provide guidelines to energy needs at various stages of life.
- Malnutrition is a result of under consumption of nutrients. Dietary disorders, anorexia and bulimia can lead to malnutrition symptoms.

Energy Intake and Expenditure

- The amount of energy calories (kcal) or kilojoules (kJ) a food contains per gram is known as its energy density.
  – Fat = 9 kcal/g; Protein = 4 kcal/g; Carbohydrate = 4 kcal/g
- What we weigh depends on the balance between how much energy we consume from our food and how much energy we use up by being physically active.
- Government guidelines state that we need to undertake 60 minutes of aerobic activity every day.
- Reference Intake (RI) is the recommended amount of each nutrient that people are required to eat daily. These replaced GDA (Guideline Daily Amounts) in some instances.

Body Mass Index

- Body Mass Index (BMI) is a measure that adults can use to see if they are a healthy weight for their height.
- The ideal healthy BMI is between 18.5 and 25.

> **Key Point**
>
> Energy balance is the balance of energy consumed through eating and drinking compared to energy burned through physical activity.

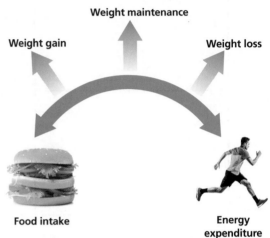

Weight maintenance · Weight gain · Weight loss · Food intake · Energy expenditure

> **Key Words**
>
> Basal Metabolic Rate (BMR)
> Physical Activity Level (PAL)
> Estimated Average Requirements (EARs)
> energy density
> Reference Intake (RI)
> Body Mass Index (BMI)

Quick Test
1. What is osteoporosis?
2. Name two symptoms of anaemia.

Review Questions

Knife Skills

1 A chef needs to have their own set of knives. Name and describe **three** different chef knives, giving one possible use for each. [9]

Name of Knife	Description	One Possible Use

Fish

1 What sign would indicate that a fish is **not** good quality? Tick (✓) **one** answer. [1]

a) Bright eyes ☐   b) Thin layer of clear slime ☐

c) Firm flesh ☐   d) Offensive odour ☐

2 Which of the following statements is **true**? Tick (✓) **one** answer. [1]

a) Fish takes a long time to cook. ☐

b) Fresh fish should have red gills. ☐

c) Fish cannot be fried without using a coating. ☐

d) Fish contains a lot of carbohydrate. ☐

3 Explain **three** ways in which fish can be preserved commercially and give **one** example of each.   [6]

Method	Example

4 Which **two** methods of preserving fish involve removing moisture from the fish?   [2]

5 Name **four** nutrients found in oily fish.   [4]

1 ....   3 ....

2 ....   4 ....

Meat

1 What temperature should pork be cooked to in order for it to be safe to eat? Tick (✓) **one** answer.   [1]

a) 63 °C ☐   b) 72 °C ☐   c) 74 °C ☐   d) 75 °C ☐

2 What causes meat to become firm when cooked? Tick (✓) **one** answer.   [1]

a) Non-enzymic browning ☐   b) Coagulation ☐

c) Maillard reaction ☐   d) Gelatinisation ☐

3 State which type of meat comes from these animals:

a) Pig ....   [1]

b) Cattle ....   [1]

c) Sheep ....   [1]

d) Deer ....   [1]

e) Poultry ....   [1]

4 Name **three** nutrients that are found in meat. [3]

....

....

....

5 Explain **three** ways to ensure that raw meat is stored safely. [6]

....

....

....

Prepare, Combine and Shape

1 What type of binding agent is generally used in a sausage mixture? Tick (✓) **one** answer. [1]

   a) Breadcrumbs ☐   **b)** Flour ☐   **c)** Egg ☐   **d)** Water ☐

2 What is the correct term given for the vegetables shown? Tick (✓) **one** answer. [1]

   a) Jardinière ☐   **b)** Julienne ☐

   c) Macedoine ☐   **d)** Brunoise ☐

3 Which of these dishes uses **three** methods of combining, shaping and coating? Tick (✓) **one** answer. [1]

   a) Burgers ☐   **b)** Fishcakes ☐

   c) Chicken goujons ☐   **d)** Koftas ☐

4 What kind of glaze is used on a batch of scones? [1]

....

5 Give **two** examples of foods that can be shaped using a mould. [2]

.... and ....

6 What is the advantage of using cutters and a rolling pin when making a batch of biscuits? [2]

....

Dough

1   Which of the following dishes would you **not** make using choux pastry? Tick (✓) **one** answer.   [1]

    a)   Eclairs ☐   **b)**   Gougère ☐

    c)   Choux buns ☐   **d)**   Bakewell tart ☐

2   Complete the following questions to show your understanding of shortcrust pastry.

    a)   What is the ratio of fat:flour? ....   [1]

    b)   What type of flour should be used? ....   [1]

    c)   What fats should be used?

         ....   [2]

    d)   What method should be used? ....   [1]

    e)   What texture should the cooked pastry have? ....   [1]

3   What are the functions of each of the following ingredients in bread dough?

    a)   Yeast ....   [1]

    b)   Sugar ....   [1]

    c)   Fat ....   [1]

    d)   Warm liquid ....   [1]

4   Why does pasta dough need to be 'rested' after kneading?   [2]

    ....

    ....

5   Which type of wheat flour is best for making a pasta dough? Tick (✓) **one** answer.   [1]

    a)   White ☐   **b)**   Wholemeal ☐

    c)   Durum ☐   **d)**   Granary ☐

Practice Questions

Protein and Fat

1 What are the main functions of protein in the diet? Tick (✓) **one** answer.　[1]

　　a) Healthy teeth and strengthening bones　☐

　　b) To support the absorption of iron　☐

　　c) Growth, maintenance and repair　☐

　　d) For a healthy digestive system　☐

2 Which of the following is a good source of High Biological Value protein? Tick (✓) **one** answer.　[1]

　　a) Lentils　☐　　b) Cheese　☐

　　c) Baked beans　☐　　d) Bread　☐

3 Give **one** example of how protein foods can be combined to complement each other.　[1]

_____

4 Which of the following is a function of fat in the diet? Tick (✓) **one** answer.　[1]

　　a) Repair of body cells　☐　　b) Insulation and warmth　☐

　　c) Protects enamel on teeth　☐　　d) Makes connective tissue　☐

5 Name **two** foods which contain saturated fatty acids.　[2]

_____

Carbohydrate

1 What is the name given to the production of carbohydrates by plants? Tick (✓) **one** answer.　[1]

　　a) Cholesterol　☐　　b) Hydrogenation　☐

　　c) Photosynthesis　☐　　d) Marinade　☐

2 Give **three** good sources of starchy carbohydrates.　[3]

_____

_____

3 Explain why the body needs carbohydrates. [2]

....

....

....

4 Dietary fibre is also known as: [1]

N .... S .... P ....

5 Give **three** good sources of dietary fibre in the diet. [3]

....

....

Vitamins

1 Which are the water-soluble vitamins? [2]

....

2 Which food is a good source of vitamin C? Tick (✓) **one** answer. [1]

a) Bread ☐   **b)** Oily fish ☐   **c)** Oranges ☐   **d)** Butter ☐

3 Explain how the loss of water-soluble vitamins can be reduced when preparing and cooking fresh vegetables. [4]

....

....

....

....

....

4 What type of vitamins are vitamins A, D, E and K? [1]

....

Practice Questions

5   Apart from dietary sources, how else does the body obtain vitamin D?   [2]

Minerals and Water

1   Name the condition caused by a lack of iron in the diet. Tick (✓) **one** answer.   [1]

    a) Scurvy ☐   **b)** Anaemia ☐   **c)** Beri-beri ☐   **d)** Dermatitis ☐

2   Milk contains calcium. Name **two** other good sources of calcium in the diet.   [2]

3   What is the function of iron in the body?   [2]

4   Name **two** good sources of iron in the diet.   [2]

5   Give **three** reasons why water is an important part of a healthy diet.   [3]

Making Informed Choices

1   Complete the sentence.   [1]

    The **E** _____ **G** _____ shows the types and proportions of the main food groups that are needed for a healthy balanced diet.

2   Eating less salt and less fat are two of the current healthy eating guidelines. List **three** other healthy eating guidelines.   [3]

3 What term is used to describe the gradual introduction of solid foods into a baby's diet? [1]

4 What does the yellow group on the Eatwell Guide show? [1]

Diet, Nutrition and Health

1 Which group of people require an increased supply of iron? Tick (✓) **one** answer. [1]

a) New-born babies ☐   **b)** Teenage girls ☐

c) Elderly men ☐   **d)** Someone working in an office. ☐

2 What is the maximum daily recommended amount of salt? Tick (✓) **one** answer. [1]

a) 2 g ☐   **b)** 6 g ☐   **c)** 16 g ☐   **d)** 24 g ☐

3 Obesity is linked to many other health conditions. Name **two** of these conditions. [2]

4 People with Type 2 diabetes cannot produce enough of which hormone? [1]

5 What are the health risks of a high-fat diet? [3]

6 Explain what is meant by basal metabolic rate (BMR). [2]

Cooking of Food, Heat Transfer and Selecting Appropriate Cooking Methods

Quick Recall Quiz

You must be able to:

- Know and understand the reasons why food is cooked and how heat is transferred to food
- Know the reasons for selecting different cooking methods.

Why is Food Cooked?

- Food is cooked in order to:
  - make it safe to eat (cooking destroys microorganisms)
  - change raw food to cooked food
  - make it palatable: develop flavours; improve mouthfeel; improve texture; reduce bulk; improve colour
  - help keep quality (extend shelf life)
  - make it easier to digest
  - give variety to diet.

How is Food Cooked?

- Cooking uses heat to change texture, flavour and colour of food.
- Cooking methods are **wet** (moist), **dry**, or **fat-based**:
  - Wet methods are boiling, steaming, stewing, poaching, casseroling and braising.
  - Dry methods are baking, roasting and grilling.
  - Fat-based methods are frying and stir-frying.
- Pre-cooking methods can improve tenderness and flavour, for example, a marinade for meat or fish.
- The selection of a cooking method depends on:
  - the type of food being cooked
  - the time available
  - the skill of the cook and the facilities available
  - the need to achieve desired characteristics, e.g. browning
  - the need to conserve vitamins, e.g. steam rather than boil to prevent loss of vitamins
  - the desire to improve palatability, varying the appearance, colour, flavour, texture and smell.

> **Key Point**
>
> Cooking food makes it safe, allows it to keep for longer and makes it more palatable.

Microwave Cooking

- Microwave cooking uses a type of radiation called microwaves, which travel in straight lines and penetrate the food.
- The microwaves vibrate water molecules creating friction, which makes heat.
- **Hot spots** can occur, so food should be stirred and left to stand to allow the heat to be distributed evenly.
- Microwaves alone do not brown or crisp foods.

Summary of Cooking Methods

Method	Characteristics	Examples
Water-based		
Boiling	softens	vegetables, rice, soup
Simmering	tenderises, evaporates	stews, vegetables, curries
Poaching	tenderises	fish, chicken, eggs
Braising	tenderises, softens	meats, fish, vegetables
Steaming	tenderises	vegetables, rice
Oven		
Moist or fat	tenderises	vegetables, joints of meat, potatoes
Dry		
Grilling/BBQ	chars, browns, crisps	bacon, toast, cheese
Baking	browns, crisps	cakes, pastries, potatoes
Dry frying	browns, crisps	bacon, lardons, chorizo, nuts
Roasting	browns, crisps	roast chicken, potatoes
Fat-based		
Deep frying	browns, crisps	battered fish, doughnuts
Shallow frying	sets, browns	eggs, onions, fish
Stir frying	softens, reduces bulk	bean sprouts, sliced vegetables

Key Point

Cooking methods can achieve specific characteristics in food.

Key Point

Heat is transferred by conduction, convection and radiation. Cooking commonly uses a combination of heat transfer methods.

Conduction

Heat Transfer

- There are three ways in which heat is transferred through food:

Conduction	Convection	Radiation
- Food molecules vibrate to transfer heat via **conduction**. - Heat is transferred by contact of heat source to pan to food, e.g. frying.	- **Convection** takes place in air (in ovens) or liquids. - Currents occur as heated air or water rises and cooler air or water falls, e.g. boiling water.	- Heat energy passing in direct lines to the food, e.g. grill to food. - Energy from microwaves penetrate food to transfer energy.

Convection

Radiation

 Quick Test

1. Cooking food makes it more palatable. Is this true or false?
2. What is the main heat transfer method when boiling food?
3. How can cooking methods be classified?
4. Name **three** types of heat transfer.

 Key Words

palatability
microwave
radiation
conduction
convection

Proteins and Enzymic Browning

You must be able to:

- Understand protein denaturation and protein coagulation
- Know about the properties of protein in gluten formation
- Understand enzymic browning and oxidation in fruit and vegetables.

Quick Recall Quiz

Protein Denaturation

- **Denaturation** occurs when the structure of amino acids found in protein are altered. They change shape or unfold because chemical bonds are broken.
- Protein in foods can be denatured (altered) by heat, reduction of **pH level** (more acid), enzymes and mechanical actions. See chart below.

> **Key Point**
>
> Proteins are denatured during cooking. Egg proteins coagulate or set when they are heated.

Heat	• Cooking denatures proteins. • Denaturation occurs when the structure of amino acids found in protein changes shape after cooking – the protein molecule uncoils when cooked.
pH	• pH is the level of acidity or alkalinity in a food. • pH is measured from 1, which is very acid, to 14, which is very alkaline. • Reducing the pH by using lemon juice or vinegar in a **marinade** denatures the protein in foods to make them tender, tasty and moist.
Enzymes	• Meat tenderisers cause protein denaturation, making meat more tender. • Enzymic tenderisers are in the form of papain and bromelain. Papain can be found naturally in papaya and bromelain can be found in fresh pineapple. • Acidic pH from yoghurt, buttermilk, vinegar or citrus fruits helps to tenderise fish or meat (marinades).
Mechanical Actions	• Whisking egg white denatures the protein by uncoiling and unfolding, e.g. foam formation occurs (gas in liquid).

Protein Coagulation

- Protein coagulation is a type of protein denaturation.
- Examples of coagulated foods are egg custards and quiches.
- It causes a change in texture, for example, runny eggs become coagulated (set).
- It usually starts at 60°C and is completed by 70°C.
- It is irreversible and causes loss of solubility.

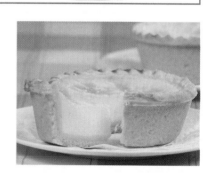

Gluten Formation

- Gluten formation occurs when water is added to a wheat flour to form a dough. Wheat flour contains two proteins, glutenin and gliadin, which combine to form gluten.
- Strong wheat flour for bread making contains more gluten than plain flour.

Gluten in Bread

- Gluten makes dough stretchy and elastic.
- Salt and kneading help strengthen gluten.
- Gluten forms the structure of a baked loaf of bread.

Gluten in Pastry

- Rubbing fat into flour makes short gluten strands – the scientific term for this is shortening.
- Gluten forms the rigid structure in baked pastry.

Gluten in Pasta Making

- Gluten in wheat flour helps pasta hold its shape, e.g. fusilli.
- Gluten also makes the pasta dough flexible and increases its ability to hold various shapes.

Proteins and Enzymic Browning

- Enzymic browing occurs on the surface of cut fruits, such as apples, and on the surface of cut vegetables, such as parsnips.
- It happens due to cell enzymes reacting with air (oxidation).
- Enzymic browning can be prevented (inhibited) by:
  - blanching cut fruits or vegetables in boiling water
  - blanching vegetables before freezing, which inhibits the enzymic action that can discolour food
  - dipping fruit or vegetables in acid, e.g. lemon juice
  - removal of air by submerging in water
  - cooking, e.g. stewing fruit, roasting parsnips.

Oxidation

- Oxidation causes discolouration, e.g. cut lettuce leaves turn pink-brown.
- Oxidation also causes vitamins to be lost, particularly vitamin C.
- Oxidation enables enzyme activity, e.g. browning, discolouration.
- Oxidation can be reduced during preparation and cooking by:
  - cooking vegetables in small amounts of water
  - using a quicker, shorter method of cooking, e.g. steaming, stir fry
  - serving vegetables immediately after cooking
  - keeping the lid on when boiling vegetables
  - using the cooking water in gravy.

> **Key Point**
>
> Enzymes can cause the browning of fruit and vegetables. Fruit and vegetables need careful handling during preparation to prevent enzymic browning.

> **Quick Test**
>
> 1. What causes the browning of cut fruit or vegetables?
> 2. What is the term used to explain the way heat changes the texture of egg proteins?

> **Key Words**
>
> denaturation
> pH level
> marinade
> enzymic browning
> oxidation

Carbohydrates

You must be able to:

- Understand the functional and chemical properties of carbohydrates, which are gelatinisation, dextrinisation and caramelisation.

Gelatinisation

- **Gelatinisation** occurs when starches (wheatflour, cornflour or arrowroot) thicken liquids. The process needs heat and agitation (stirring), especially in sauce making. It occurs during the cooking of starchy food such as potatoes, rice or pasta.

Gelatinisation in Sauce Making

- When thickening a sauce, gelatinisation occurs.
- Starch grains absorb liquid, swell, burst (at 80°C) and finally thicken a sauce. Starches complete thickening at just under 100°C, so it is important to cook to boiling point to avoid a sauce with a raw taste.
- Sauces need stirring (agitating) to prevent lumps forming, to stop the sauce from sticking to the bottom of the pan and to aid heat transfer during the process of gelatinisation.
- Basic recipes use different methods and different thickening agents, as seen when using the roux method, the blending method and the all-in-one method.

Gelatinisation and Ratios

- A sauce is viscous, which means it can either be poured (e.g. parsley sauce) or used to coat an ingredient (e.g. cauliflower cheese) or to bind other dry ingredients together (e.g. rissoles).
- The change in **viscosity** is due to the ratio of thickening agent to liquid; more starch gives a thicker sauce. The ratio selected changes the **consistency** of the sauce from runny to thick.
- Retrogradation is the deterioration of a starch-based sauce on keeping – this results in shrinkage, drying and cracking.
- Syneresis is the loss of fluid from a foam or set mixture, e.g. lemon meringue pie, and in cheese making.

> ### Key Point
>
> Gelatinisation is the function of starches as thickening agents.

Modified Starches and Gelatinisation

- Modified starches are used to help gelatinisation occur in different ways. Quick-cook pasta or rice are modified by pre-gelatinisation.
- Milkshakes use starch modified to allow cold liquid thickening.
- Instant thickening granules are modified starch that can be sprinkled into boiling liquids.

- Modified starches thicken cold desserts without the application of heat, and are used to thicken and stabilise salad dressings.

Dextrinisation

- **Dextrinisation** occurs when starch is toasted or cooked by dry heat, e.g. toasted or charred bread.
- It is a result of starch breakdown by dry heat to form dextrins.
- It changes the properties of starch as a result of heat application.
- Dextrinisation is known as non-enzymic browning.
- Dextrins taste sweeter than starch and add flavour to toasted, charred or baked goods.
- Dextrins are hygroscopic, absorbing moisture from the air, e.g. toasted or baked products soften slightly on keeping. Baked produce is best stored in an airtight tin or container with lid.
- Characteristics of dextrinisation are golden colours, browning, sweeter taste and crispness.

Caramelisation

- **Caramelisation** causes sugar to change colour and flavour due to dry or moist heat.
- It causes surface browning on baked goods containing sugar.
- It changes the properties of sugar; solutions become syrups.
- It is known as non-enzymic browning.
- Characteristics of caramelisation are a golden colour, browning, gloss, sweetness and stickiness.

Examples of Caramelisation (Browning) in Food Preparation

- Frying onions, or frying or roasting parsnips, potatoes or squash.
- Making a crème brulee or crème caramel.
- Spun sugar caramelisation is created through the application of **dry** heat to sugar.
- Fudge, toffee or halva are created through the application of **wet** heat to caramelise the sugar.
- Preparing glazed pork ribs or chicken wings.

Browning and Carbohydrates

- Dry methods of cooking gradually turn starches and sugars golden brown. This aids the palatability of the products by improving flavour, texture and colour.
- Browning is often used as an indicator of adequate cooking e.g. cook until golden brown.

 Key Point

Sauces can be different thicknesses when the proportion of ingredients is altered.

 Key Point

Dextrinisation is the term used to describe browning of starch caused by heat. Caramelisation is the browning of sugars caused by heat.

 Key Words

gelatinisation
viscosity
consistency
dextrinisation
caramelisation

Quick Test

1. What term describes thickening a sauce using starch?
2. What sort of heat transfer commonly causes dextrinisation?
3. Dextrins attract and absorb moisture from the air. Is this true or false?

Quick Recall Quiz

Fats and Oils

You must be able to:

- Understand the role of fats and oils in shortening, plasticity, aeration and emulsification
- Know the functional and chemical properties of fats and oils.

Types of Fat

- Fat from animal sources include butter and lard – these are saturated fats.
- Fat from vegetable sources include margarine and vegetable shortening – these are unsaturated fats and are suitable for vegetarians, vegans and certain religions.

Shortening

- **Shortening** is a process using fat that creates a characteristic short, crumbly texture.
- Shortening is seen in shortcrust pastry, shortbread biscuits, cookies and rich pastries.
- The process in food preparation most likely to bring about shortening is the rubbing-in method.

How Does a Fat Shorten a Pastry Mixture?

- Fats with plasticity are good shortening agents because they rub-in easily.
- Fat coats the flour grains, preventing gluten development.
- The cooked texture is short and crumbly.

What Happens During the Cooking of Pastry?

- The flour grains absorb the fat.
- Pastry changes from pliable to rigid (the gluten sets).
- Pastry turns golden brown.

Plasticity

- **Plasticity** means the ability of a fat to change properties over a range of temperatures. Temperature is an important factor in plasticity of fats.
- Cold fats are solid and firm.
- Fats at room temperature become spreadable and soft.
- Plasticity means fats such as butter can be used for spreading, rubbing-in, creaming, melting-method cooking or for muffins.
- Warmed fats melt and become runny.

> **Key Point**
>
> Fats make pastry short and crumbly. Fats give colour and flavour to pastry. The plasticity of fat allows it to be used for rubbing-in, spreading and creaming.

Aeration

- **Aeration** helps products have a light and open texture.
- Fats aerate mixtures during beating or **creaming** with sugar.
- Aeration increases the volume of a product by incorporating air.
- Beating, whipping, creaming and whisking are methods that help aeration.
- During preparation of a creamed mixture:
  - the fat and sugar are creamed together, trapping air (aeration)
  - the mixture becomes paler
  - an air-in-fat **foam** is formed.
- During baking:
  - trapped air expands
  - the cake rises.

Emulsions

- Emulsions are mixtures of liquids that do not normally mix (known as 'immiscible' liquids), e.g. oil and water.
- Emulsifiers have a hydrophilic end, which is water-loving and forms chemical bonds with water, and a hydrophobic end, which is water-hating and forms chemical bonds with oil.
- Fats and oils add texture, flavour and colour to emulsified sauces such as Hollandaise, which is a hot emulsion, and mayonnaise, which is a cold emulsion.
- Stabilisers keep emulsions mixed, preventing them separating.

Types of emulsions

Oil-in-water   Water-in-oil

The Process of Emulsification
- **Emulsification** requires agitation by whisking, by mixer or food processor.
- It requires slow addition of oil to prevent the emulsion splitting.
- Emulsification is helped by a natural emulsifier called lecithin, which is present in egg yolks.
- A good example of emulsification is seen when making mayonnaise, a smooth, stable emulsion for salad dressing.
- Vinaigrette dressing (oil and vinegar) is not a stable emulsion – it will separate out on standing.

Oil and balsamic vinegar

Quick Test

1. What term describes how fat makes a short texture product?
2. The ability of a fat to change properties is known as plasticity. Is this true or false?
3. Which basic cake-making process traps air into the cake?

Raising Agents

You must be able to:

- Understand the processes of raising or aerating using physical and mechanical methods
- Know and understand the working properties of chemical and biological raising agents.

Raising and Aerating

Physical Methods	Mechanical Methods
• **Physical raising methods** such as air, water vapour or steam help products to have a light, open texture. • Recipes that need to be light have ingredients that function as raising agents such as water, milk or egg whites.	• Food preparation methods such as sieving, whisking or beating can be used to trap air. • Combinations of physical and mechanical methods work well in food preparation to make mixtures light, e.g. batters for Yorkshire puddings.

Air, Steam and Foam as Raising Agents

- **Air** is a very effective raising agent because it expands when it is heated. Air pockets swell and volume increases.
- Food preparation techniques help prevent loss of air, e.g. folding in flour when making a whisked sponge cake.
- **Steam** is produced from water in a mixture; this is a physical change.
- Steam produces light, open and uneven textures and adds volume during cooking, e.g. profiteroles.
- Moist mixtures produce steam during cooking.
- **Foams** - whisking helps trap air, creating foam.
- Ingredients containing protein form foams, e.g. milk froth, egg whites, aquafaba.
- Egg whites stretch and unravel to trap air to form a gas-in-liquid foam.
- Sugar stabilises foam, e.g. cold-set soufflé.
- Egg white foams set mousses.
- Cooking stabilises foam, e.g. roulade, meringue.

Chemical Raising Agents

- Chemical raising agents produce carbon dioxide when heated with a liquid.
- They cause effervescent fizzing and bubbles of gas.
- Chemical raising agents must be carefully measured.

Bicarbonate of Soda

- Bicarbonate of soda is an alkaline powder.
- It can leave a soapy aftertaste but strong flavours, e.g. gingerbread, will mask the aftertaste.
- It works more effectively with an acid ingredient such as buttermilk or cream of tartar, e.g. soda bread.
- The acid neutralises the alkali and prevents a soapy aftertaste.
- Cream of tartar is an acid raising agent, which is frequently used alongside bicarbonate of soda, e.g. in scones.

Baking Powder

- Baking powder is a ready-to-use mixture of cream of tartar plus bicarbonate of soda and rice flour.

Self Raising Flour

- Self-raising flour is plain flour with baking powder added during manufacture. Plain flour does not contain a raising agent.
- Self-raising flour can be brown or white.
- Self-raising flour contains a pre-sieved precisely measured amount of baking powder for ease and speed of use.

Gingerbread

Biological Raising Agents

- **Yeast** is a biological raising agent. It ferments to give off carbon dioxide gas.
- Fermentation in yeast is a **biological** (also known as biotechnological) **raising agent**.
- The conditions for yeast fermentation are warm temperature 25°C–35°C; moisture; food; time.
- Temperatures above 60°C during baking will inactivate and finally destroy yeast cells.
- Yeast is the raising agent in bread, bread rolls, buns and rich pastries (Danish pastries).
- Leavened bread contains raising agent in the form of yeast or bicarbonate of soda.
- Unleavened bread contains no raising agent and is flat in structure.

> **Key Point**
>
> Gas and air bubbles expand on heating to make a product rise.

> **Quick Test**
>
> 1. What is the raising agent in a whisked sponge cake?
> 2. What happens when air is heated?
> 3. How does egg white trap air?
> 4. How can water help make a mixture light during cooking?

> **Key Words**
>
> physical raising methods
> chemical raising agents
> yeast
> biological raising agent

Review Questions

Protein and Fat

1 (Circle) **three** foods that contain High Biological Value (HBV) protein. [3]

bread   chicken   grapes   butter

milk   broccoli   soya   lentils

2 What is it called when Low Biological Value (LBV) protein foods are eaten together to provide a good supply of all the essential amino acids? [1]

3 Over-consumption of saturated fat foods is likely to raise what level in the body? [1]

Carbohydrate

1 Unscramble the following starchy carbohydrate foods. [3]

astap

ototpa

otsa

2 Anyone suffering from constipation needs to eat more foods high in dietary fibre/non-starch polysaccharide (NSP). <u>Underline</u> **four** foods that are high in NSP. [4]

cornflakes   lentils   cabbage   cream crackers

eggs   apples   shredded wheat   milk

3 Which type of carbohydrate is linked to tooth decay? [1]

Vitamins

1 Circle three foods that are a good source of Vitamin C (ascorbic acid). [3]

      cheese   **sardines**   **kiwi fruit**   **peanut butter**

            lemons   **margarine**   **cabbage**

2 Explain why a pregnant woman needs an increased intake of folate (folic acid). [1]

3 Give **two** reasons why raw vegetables contain more vitamins than cooked vegetables. [2]

4 What is the alternative name for Vitamin C? [1]

Minerals and Water

1 Fill in the missing words. [3]

Iron supports the production of .... in ....

.... cells; this transports .... around the body.

2 Why is iron-deficiency anaemia common in teenage girls? [1]

3 Iodine is a component of thyroid hormones. What do these hormones regulate in the body? [1]

4 Give **two** reasons why someone may need to increase their water intake. [2]

_____

_____

Making Informed Choices

1 Which of the following foods would you serve to a teenage girl to increase her intake of iron? Circle **three** foods. [3]

oranges   chocolate   digestive biscuits

beef   apricots   salad

2 What is the Eatwell Guide? Tick (✓) **one** answer. [1]

a) A chart that shows you how long foods can be kept for. ☐

b) A guide that informs you of where to shop for the healthiest food. ☐

c) A guide that shows the proportions of food groups that should be eaten daily for a well-balanced diet. ☐

d) A guide that tells you how long foods have to be reheated. ☐

3 Fill in the missing words. [2]

Babies are born with a supply of i_____ stored in the l_____.

Diet, Nutrition and Health

1 What is obesity? Tick (✓) **one** answer. [1]

a) abnormal accumulation of body fat ☐

b) lack of thyroid hormone ☐

c) weakened teeth and gums ☐

d) narrowing of the arteries ☐

2 Which of the following foods would you serve to an elderly person to keep their bones as healthy as possible? (Circle) **three** foods. [3]

oranges　　　　milky drinks　　　　digestive biscuits

sausages　　　　cheese　　　　yoghurts　　　　salad

3 How does someone with diabetes manage the condition? [2]

....

....

....

4 What is a healthy BMI for adults? Tick (✓) **one** answer. [1]

a) 7.5–12 ☐

b) 13.5–18 ☐

c) 18.5–25 ☐

d) 32–38.5 ☐

5 What is osteoporosis? [1]

....

....

....

Practice Questions

Cooking of Food, Heat Transfer and Selecting Appropriate Cooking Methods

1 Show you understand the key reasons for cooking food. Complete the following statements using the words in the boxes below.

shelf life	digest	variety	microorganisms	keep quality

Food is cooked to:

a) make it safe to eat by destroying ....　　[1]

b) help extend .... and ....　　[2]

c) improve .... in the diet.　　[1]

d) make it easier to ....　　[1]

2 Name **three** methods of heat transfer.　　[3]

....　　..　　..

3 Listed below are the three classifications of cooking methods. Name **two** examples of each classification.　　[6]

	Water-based Methods	Dry Cooking Methods	Fat-based Methods
Example 1			
Example 2			

Proteins and Enzymic Browning

1 Protein foods can be denatured in four ways. What are the **four** ways?　　[4]

....

....

2   During the cooking of a quiche the egg filling changes texture.

    a) In what way does the texture of the quiche filling change during baking?   [1]

    b) Why does the texture of the quiche filling change during baking?   [2]

3   **a)** What is the name of the protein in wheat flour?   [1]

    b) In what way is the protein content of strong flour different to plain cake flour?   [1]

4   **a)** State **two** actions that are required for wheat flour to form gluten.   [2]

    b) Gluten is formed from two proteins in wheat; glutenin is one, what is the other protein?   [1]

5   **a)** What is the term used to explain browning in foods not as a result of either dextrinisation or caramelisation?   [1]

    b) Explain one way to prevent enzymic browning when using apples.   [1]

Carbohydrates

1 Circle the correct words in the following passage. [5]

The function of starch in thickening a **solid / liquid** is known as **gelatinisation / caramelisation**. For a sauce to thicken it needs to be **chilled / heated** and also **stirred / sieved** to ensure a smooth sauce. A sauce should be heated to **setting point / boiling point** to prevent it tasting raw.

2 **a)** As bread is toasted dextrins are formed. How does dextrin affect the colour, flavour and texture of toast slices? [3]

Colour ....

Flavour ....

Texture ....

b) What is the scientific term for the effect of dry heat on starch? [1]

....

c) Dextrins attract moisture from the air. What is the scientific term for this? [1]

....

d) How does this process affect the quality of the toast? [1]

....

Fats and Oils

1 Which of these statements is **not** true? Tick (✓) one answer. [1]

a) Shortening is a process that creates a hard texture in products. ☐

b) Shortening is seen in shortcrust pastry, shortbread biscuits, cookies and rich pastries. ☐

c) The process in food preparation most likely to bring about shortening is the rubbing-in method. ☐

2 Fats are used in food preparation to promote characteristic textures, flavours and colours. Identify the functional properties of fat in the preparation processes on the following page. [6]

Process	Function of Process	End Product Characteristic
a) Fat and sugar beaten (creamed) together in a mixture	Explain **two** functions	Give **two** characteristics
b) Margarine or butter rubbed into a flour mixture	**One** function	**One** characteristic

Raising Agents

1 Describe **three** functions of raising agents in food preparation. [3]

1 .... 2 .... 3 ....

2 A baker wants her shop assistants to understand raising agents. She uses examples from her shop.

Example 1 is a whisked sponge flan.

a) What is the raising agent in the flan sponge? [1]

....

b) Describe how the raising agent is incorporated into the sponge. [1]

....

....

Example 2 is a cheese scone.

c) Which raising agent is used in scones? [1]

....

d) What gas would the raising agent produce? [1]

....

e) Explain how the raising agent works during baking. [2]

....

....

Microorganisms, Enzymes and Food Spoilage

Quick Recall Quiz

You must be able to:

- Know the growth conditions for microorganisms and enzymes and the control of food spoilage
- Know and understand that bacteria, yeasts and moulds are microorganisms
- Explain that enzymes are biological catalysts usually made from protein.

Bacteria

- **Bacteria** are small single-celled organisms that are able to reproduce rapidly. They are also called **microorganisms.**
- Bacteria can be harmful (pathogenic) and cause food poisoning but can also be useful as in the production of cheese and yoghurt.

Conditions for Growth

Temperature	• Bacteria generally multiply between 5 °C and 63 °C. • The average ideal temperature for rapid bacterial multiplication is 37 °C, which is body temperature.
Moisture	• Bacteria need moisture to live and multiply.

Time	• Under optimum conditions, bacteria will multiply every 10–20 minutes, so within seven hours one bacterium can become one million.
	 • To control bacteria multiplying:
	   – eat food as soon as possible after making/cooking
	   – if food is not being eaten straight away, cool down as quickly as possible (within 90 minutes is recommended) and store in the fridge or freezer. A blast chiller will cool food more quickly than the recommended 90 minutes.

Nutrients	• Bacteria can multiply to large numbers on high-risk foods such as meat, poultry, fish, eggs and milk.
pH level	• Bacteria grow best at a neutral pH level, between 6.6 and 7.5. • Bacteria are unable to survive below pH 4.5. • Vinegar (acetic acid) has a pH of 3.5.

Yeast

- Yeast are single-celled plants found in the air and on skins of fruit.
- Yeast spoils the taste of food but is not harmful.
- It grows only on sugary foods, but not in sugar concentrations above 50% (jams should be made with 60% sugar).
- It can survive without air.
- It can't grow at low temperatures or survive in vinegar.
- It is destroyed at temperatures above 70 °C.

> **Key Point**
>
> Bacteria are found everywhere and need the right temperature, warmth, time, nutrients, pH level and oxygen to grow and multiply.

Revise

- Yeast is a very helpful organism. It is used in baking bread, where carbon dioxide is used as a raising agent, and in wine making and brewing.

Moulds

- **Moulds** are a type of fungus, that settle on food and grow into a visible plant.
- Moulds grow on many foods, such as bread, cheese and meat.
- They like slightly acidic conditions.
- They need moisture and warmth (20 °C–40 °C), but are destroyed by heat <70 °C.
- Moulds can survive in the fridge but not in the freezer.
- Mould on food is a sign that it is not very fresh or has been stored incorrectly. Some mould can result in allergic reaction and respiratory difficulties.

Enzymes

- **Enzymes** in food can be a problem for food storage.
- The cells break open, the enzymes escape and react with other parts of the food. Soft spots appear on fruit and vegetables and makes meat smell and taste bad.
- Denaturing the enzymes can help to preserve the food, e.g. through heat, use of acids, strong alkalis or salt.
- Enzymes are chemical catalysts that are found in all cells.
- Enzymes break down plant and animal tissues, causing fruit to ripen, meat to tenderise and enzymic browning (also known as oxidation) to speed up.

Ways to Prevent Oxidation (Enzymic Browning)

- Adding lemon juice (an acid) to a fruit salad prevents browning.
- Blanching vegetables before freezing prevents discolouration.
- Removing air by immersing potatoes in water will prevent browning.
- Refrigeration or freezing will slow down browning.
- The removal of moisture (dehydration) will prevent browning, however it is a slow process and the browning reaction is quick.

 Quick Test

1. What are microorganisms?
2. What is the ideal temperature for bacterial growth?
3. How can we control bacterial growth?
4. Name **two** food products that use yeast.

Key Words

bacteria
microorganisms
moulds
enzymes

Microorganisms, Enzymes and Food Spoilage : Revise   59

Microorganisms in Food Production

You must be able to:

- Demonstrate knowledge and understanding of the use of microorganisms in food production, including moulds in the production of blue cheese, yeasts as a raising agent in bread and the use of bacteria in yoghurt production.

The Dairy Industry

- It would be impossible to make cheese without a starter culture.
- As the culture grows in the milk, it converts the sugar lactose into lactic acid, which ensures the correct level of acidity and gives the cheese its moisture.
- As the cheese ripens, the culture gives it a balanced aroma, taste, and texture.
- Choosing the right mixture of culture is essential for a high-quality cheese.

Cheese Production and Moulds

- Cheeses that rely on moulds for their characteristic properties include:
  - blue cheese (such as blue stilton and roquefort)
  - soft ripened cheese (such as camembert and brie)
  - rind-washed cheese (such as époisses and taleggio).

Blue Cheese

- To make blue cheese:
  - the cheese is treated with a mould
  - as the cheese matures, the mould grows
  - this creates blue veins within the cheese, giving the cheese its characteristic flavour, e.g. stilton and roquefort.

Blue cheese

Soft Ripened Cheese

- To make soft ripened cheese:
  - P. camemberti is allowed to grow on the outside of the cheese, causing the cheese to age from the outside in, forming a soft white crust and runny inside e.g. brie and camembert.

Soft ripened cheese

Rind-washed Cheese

- To make rind-washed cheeses:
  - rind-washed cheeses also ripen inwards but they are washed with brine and other ingredients, e.g. beer and wine, which contain mould
  - this makes them attractive to bacteria, which adds to the flavour, e.g. limburger.

Rind-washed cheese

Yoghurt

- In yoghurt, the culture is responsible for the taste and texture of the final product.
- In recent years **probiotic** cultures have become popular in dairy products because of their health benefits.
- Probiotic cultures are carefully selected strains, and there is good evidence that they help improve digestion, safeguard the immune system, and keep the body's intestinal flora in balance.
- Probiotic cultures are classified as a functional food.

The Meat Industry

- Meat starter cultures are used to make dried, fermented products such as salami, pepperoni, chorizo and dried ham.
- Lactic bacteria develop the flavour and colour of the products.
- A wide variety of moulds are used to ripen the surface of sausages, preserving the natural quality of the product and controlling the development of flavour.

Yeast

- Yeast is used in bread-making as well as in making beer and wine.
- Yeast is a microorganism.
- Yeast requires sugar to grow.
- In bread making, yeast will:
  - leaven the dough by producing CO_2
  - through fermentation and its enzymic action on other ingredients, create a stretchy dough
  - contribute to the flavour of the bread.

> ### Key Point
>
> Microorganisms (bacteria) are used to make a wide range of food products. Bacteria are used to make cheese, yoghurt, and bread. The most important bacteria in food manufacturing are the Lactobacillus species.

Quick Test

1. What is the most important bacteria used in food manufacturing?
2. What is blue cheese treated with to give it its taste and texture?
3. In what ways are probiotic cultures considered to have health benefits?

> ### Key Words
>
> starter culture
> probiotic

Bacterial Contamination

Quick Recall Quiz

You must be able to:

- Know and understand the different sources of bacterial contamination
- Know and understand the main types of bacteria that cause food-poisoning
- Demonstrate knowledge and understanding of the main sources and methods of control of different food-poisoning bacteria types
- Recognise the general symptoms of food poisoning.

Bacteria

- Bacteria can be found everywhere, including raw food, people, air and dust, equipment and utensils, soil, pests, water and food waste.

The Dangers of Bacteria

- It is essential to control the conditions that allow bacteria to multiply and cause illness, e.g. stick to strict time and temperature controls.
- You can become ill if you eat food that is contaminated by certain bacteria (pathogens) and viruses.
- Kitchens provide the ideal conditions for bacteria growth.
- Bacteria are microscopic. You cannot tell if a food is contaminated by just looking at it.

Food-poisoning Bacteria

- Food poisoning is caused by bacteria multiplying in or on food.

Pathogenic Bacteria	Foods Affected	Symptoms	Onset	Special Note
Salmonella	Raw meat; Eggs; Seafood; Dairy products	Diarrhoea; Vomiting; Fever	12–36 hours	May be fatal to the elderly and babies; Found in human and animal excreta
Staphylococcus Aureus	Cooked sliced meat; Dairy products; Anything touched by hand	Vomiting; Diarrhoea; Abdominal pain	1–6 hours	Present in nasal passages, throat and skin; Associated with dirty food handlers; Good personal hygiene is crucial
Clostridium perfingens	Raw and cooked meat and meat products	Nausea; Diarrhoea; Abdominal pain	8–22 hours	
Clostridium Botulinum	Incorrectly canned meat, fish or vegetables	Paralysis; Difficulty breathing; Double vision; Nausea; Vomiting	12–48 hours	Rare
Bacillus cereus	Cooked rice, pasta and cereal foods	Nausea; Vomiting; Diarrhoea	1–6 hours	

Food-borne Disease

- Food-borne diseases are caused by pathogenic microbes (bacteria and viruses) carried on food. These microbes do not multiply in the food but in the person who has eaten the food.

Pathogenic Microbes	Foods Affected	Symptoms	Onset	Special Note
Escherichia-Coli (E-Coli)	Raw meat; Untreated milk and water	Vomiting; Blood in diarrhoea; Kidney damage or failure	12–24 hours	Causes gastro-enteritis in humans
Listeria Monocytogenes	Soft cheeses; Pate; Unpasteurized milk; Undercooked meat; Incorrectly heated cook-chill meals	A range of symptoms from mild flu-like symptoms to septicemia, meningitis and pneumonia	No specific time	Can cause miscarriage, premature labour and birth
Campylobacter	Meat; Shellfish; Untreated water; Washing raw poultry	Diarrhoea; Headache; Fever; Abdominal pain	1–11 days	Easily transmitted between humans. Raw meat and poultry **MUST NOT** be washed as this spreads the bacteria
Norovirus	Shellfish; Raw vegetables; Salads	Nausea; Vomiting; Diarrhoea; Abdominal pain; Fever	1–2 days	Projectile vomiting The virus can survive for several days if not cleaned up properly

Preventing Contamination

- Preventing contamination is the key to food safety.
- Keep the kitchen clean and tidy. Clean and disinfect all areas, equipment and utensils used to prepare food.
- Keep food covered. Handle the food as little as possible.
- Store food correctly. Cook food thoroughly.
- Remove food waste and rubbish.

Food Poisoning

- Food poisoning is caused by harmful bacteria multiplying in or on food.
- Symptoms usually pass in a few days and the sufferer will make a full recovery.
- Food poisoning can affect anyone, but some people may suffer more than others, such as very young children and babies; elderly people; those who have had a serious illness or are recovering from a serious illness; pregnant women and nursing mothers; people who have allergies.

> **Key Point**
>
> Bacterial contamination is the presence of harmful bacteria in our food, which can lead to food poisoning and illness. As a food handler, you must do everything possible to prevent this contamination.

> **Quick Test**
>
> 1. What are the main symptoms of food poisoning?
> 2. Name **three** bacteria responsible for food poisoning.
> 3. What are the typical sources of food poisoning?
> 4. Which groups of people are more at risk of food poisoning?

> **Key Words**
>
> pathogens
> food poisoning
> contamination

Buying and Storing Food

Quick Recall Quiz

You must be able to:

- Know and understand the food safety principles when buying and storing food
- Know and understand temperature control and ambient storage
- Understand danger zone temperatures and be able to describe the correct uses of domestic fridges and freezers
- Understand date marks.

Buying Safe Food

- Make sure the food is safe for consumption.
- Check for signs of damage to tins, packets and packaging.
- Check the date marks – the **use-by date** and **best-before date**.
- Stock rotation makes sure that food is used within date (when it is safe) and prevents unnecessary waste.

Use-by Dates

- A use-by date is a safety date found on foods and their packaging.
- Use-by dates are found on highly perishable, packaged food such as meat, fish and dairy products that require chilling and have a short shelf life.
- It is an offence for businesses to sell or use food that has passed its use-by date.

Best-before Dates

- Best-before dates usually appear on less perishable foods that have a long shelf life, such as canned, dried and **frozen food** products.

Storing Food

- It is important to store food properly.
- Food should be wrapped, covered or kept in a suitable clean container.
- Raw meat, poultry, fish and eggs should always be stored away from ready-to-eat foods. Raw vegetables, including salad leaves, may contain pathogens from the soil and should be kept away from ready-to-eat/high-risk foods.
- The refrigerator should be cleaned regularly.
- Dry food ingredients, e.g. dried pasta, tinned tomatoes, herbs and spices should be stored in cupboards that are clean and dry.
- Frozen food still could have bacteria present but they are dormant. Enzymes that cause food spoilage are slowed but not stopped unless inactivated – this is the reason for blanching vegetables before freezing.

- Food ingredients and finished products must be:
  - at the correct temperature
  - protected from contamination
- Food ingredients should be used according to the date marks on the food or its packaging.
- Using food within the date marks avoids waste and reduces the risk of cross contamination.

Chilled Food Storage

- Fridges should be set to operate at a temperature between 1 °C and 4 °C to make sure that **chilled food** is held below 5 °C.
- Door handles should be cleaned and disinfected.
- Raw ready-to-eat food and high-risk foods should be kept above raw food (for cooking) in the fridge.
- Food must be kept covered, and food-safe containers and food labels used.
- Never put warm food in a fridge, it will cause the temperature in the fridge to rise into the danger zone (5 °C–63 °C).

Frozen Food Storage

- Bacteria are dormant in the freezer.
- Frozen food should be stored at −18 °C or below.
- Food should be well wrapped to prevent freezer burn through loss of moisture.
- Food bought as frozen should be stored in the freezer as soon as possible.

Defrosting

- If frozen foods are not defrosted thoroughly, ice crystals remain at the centre. Cooking will melt the ice but the correct core temperature may not be achieved and bacteria may survive.
- Protect defrosting food from being contaminated.
- If high-risk food is defrosted at room temperature, bacteria will start to multiply on the surface of the food.
- Defrosted food must be treated like chilled food.

Key Point

When handling food at any stage, from buying the food through to correct storage, steps must be taken to prevent contamination. Everything possible must be done to control the conditions that allow bacteria to multiply, causing food poisoning.

Quick Test

1. What are the **two** date marks you need to check when buying food?
2. What is the recommended temperature for chilled food?
3. It is acceptable to put warm food in the fridge. True or false?
4. What is the recommended temperature for a freezer?
5. What happens to food that is not defrosted thoroughly?

Key Words

use-by date
best-before date
frozen food
chilled food

Preparing and Cooking Food

Quick Recall Quiz

You must be able to:

- Know and understand the food safety principles when preparing and cooking food, including the importance of personal hygiene and clean work surfaces
- Understand about cross contamination and temperature controls
- Know the factors surrounding high-risk food
- Demonstrate knowledge of the correct use of temperature probes.

Personal Hygiene

- Food handlers are a common source of pathogenic bacteria.
- When preparing food, you must maintain the highest possible standards of personal **hygiene** in order to avoid contaminating food and causing illness.
- A clean apron should always be worn to protect the food from contamination from your clothes.
- All jewellery should be removed when cooking, food handlers must tie back long hair or wear a hairnet/hat, and fingernails should be kept short and clean with no nail varnish.
- Licking your fingers or utensils when cooking must be avoided.
- Wash your hands:
  - before preparing food
  - between handling raw and **high-risk foods** or ready-to-eat foods
  - after you have been to the toilet
  - after sneezing/coughing
  - after changing a waterproof plaster
  - after cleaning, after handling food waste or rubbish and known allergens.

Preparing Food

- Food needs to be protected from contamination during preparation, as the food is usually uncovered while being handled.
- Food should be handled as little as possible.
- Food must be kept out of the **danger zone** (5 °C–63 °C) as bacteria will multiply.
- To prevent cross contamination, raw food and cooked food must be prepared separately using separate utensils (different chopping boards and knives). Red chopping boards and knives are used for raw meat and should only be used for this purpose.

Preparing High-risk Foods

- When preparing food, some foods are more of a risk than others: these are high-risk foods.
- Protein-based foods, moist foods and ready-to-eat foods that require no further cooking are high-risk foods.
- High-risk foods require strict time and temperature controls.

Key Points

When preparing and cooking food it is important to have high personal and food hygiene standards.

High-risk foods include:
- cold cooked meat
- poultry
- fish and seafood
- ready meals containing gravy or sauce
- egg products, such as quiche and homemade mayonnaise
- although not high in protein, cooked rice, pasta and cereals are classed as high-risk as they can provide a moist environment where certain bacteria can multiply
- dairy-based products, e.g. cream cakes and desserts.

Cooking and Reheating

- Pathogenic bacteria can be destroyed and food made safe by thorough cooking. If food is not cooked correctly, pathogenic bacteria may survive and cause food poisoning.
- To make sure bacteria are killed, the thickest part of the food (the core) should reach 70 °C for two minutes.
- Liquids should be stirred to avoid cold spots.
- Large items should be turned to ensure even cooking.
- Poultry, pork and minced meat products must be thoroughly cooked to kill the bacteria.
- If a microwave oven is to be used, always follow the manufacturer's guidelines.
- Hot holding is the process of storing food warm for service. Food must be kept at a temperature of no lower than 63 °C for a maximum of 90 minutes before being discarded.
- Food must not be **reheated** more than once.
- Bacteria will multiply during repeated cooling and reheating.
- Reheated food should reach a **core temperature** of 75 °C.

> **Key Point**
>
> Food must be cooked thoroughly to make it safe to eat.

Cleaning

- All food contact surfaces and hand contact surfaces must be cleaned and disinfected after use. Best practice is to 'clean as you go'.
- Food preparation areas must be kept clean to protect food from: bacterial contamination, physical contamination, allergenic contamination and chemical contamination.
- Food preparation areas must be kept clean to prevent slips and trips.

Types of Food Poisoning

- Food poisoning can occur through:
  - Microbiological contamination – this is the germ itself contaminating the food.
  - Physical contamination – this is when items physically drop into food, i.e. rings, nails, hair.
  - Chemical contamination – this is when chemicals get into food, i.e. cleaning chemicals.

Temperature Probes

- Temperature probes are used to take the core temperature of food.
- Care must be taken to ensure the probe does not cause cross contamination: it must be cleaned and disinfected after every use.

> **Quick Test**
>
> 1. List **four** occasions during food preparation when you must wash your hands.
> 2. What temperature control and time during cooking kills most bacteria?

> **Key Words**
>
> hygiene
> high-risk foods
> danger zone
> reheating
> core temperature

Review Questions

Cooking of Food, Heat Transfer and Selecting Appropriate Cooking Methods

1 Improving palatability is one of the main functions of food preparation and cooking. Fill in the blanks to complete the following text. [5]

Palatability means how acceptable the sensory characteristics of a food are, e.g. how

appetising it is. Making food palatable develops .... ,

improves .... and .... , reduces

.... and changes ....

2 Many methods of cooking use a combination of heat transfer. Explain how methods of heat transfer can combine when boiling potatoes. [6]

....

....

....

....

....

....

Proteins and Enzymic Browning

1 What does protein denaturation mean? Give **one** example, and explain this example (continued on page 69).

Meaning [2]

....

....

Example [2]

_____

_____

2 Choose the correct words from the boxes below to complete the sentences. [5]

elastic	kneading	short	gluten	structure

Wheat flour contains the protein _____ which makes a dough

stretchy and _____ . Different cooking techniques can affect gluten

formation, e.g. _____ helps increase gluten formation in

breadmaking, whereas rubbing fat into flour makes _____ gluten

strands to aid the texture. Gluten forms the _____ of pastries,

breads and cakes.

Carbohydrates

1 What are **two** changes that can be noticed when a solution of sugar and water is heated? [2]

_____

_____

2 Complete the boxes to give the scientific terms for changes that occur during baking. [2]

Ingredients	Effect of Baking	Scientific Term	Characteristic
Flour	Starch browns		Golden colour
Sugar	Sugars brown		Golden colour

3 Give **one** practical application of each of the scientific terms that complete the table in question 2. [2]

1 _____   2 _____

Review Questions

4 A chef is planning to use a roux sauce to coat steamed cauliflower. Which recipe would be his best choice and why?

Recipe A	Recipe B
500 ml milk	500 ml milk
10 g flour	25 g flour
10 g butter	25 g butter

a) Choice .... [1]

b) Explain your answer. [4]

....

....

Fats and Oils

1 A student decides to make shortcrust pastry by hand.

a) What is the name of the method he would use? .... [1]

b) Describe how the process makes a short textured pastry. [6]

....

....

....

....

....

....

2 Choose the correct words from the boxes below to complete the following sentences (continued on page 71). [6]

natural	emulsions	lecithin	immiscible	stable	separates

.... are mixtures of liquids that do not normally mix together.

Vinaigrette dressing is an example of an .... liquid, it

.... on standing.

Mayonnaise is an example of a .... emulsion. The

.... in egg yolks helps make emulsions stable because it is a

.... emulsifier.

3 Indicate which of the following statements are true and which are false. Circle the
correct answer. [4]

a) The plasticity of a fat enables fat to perform effectively when using the rubbing-in method.
Circle the answer.

   True   False

b) Plasticity means a fat cannot change properties. Circle the answer.

   True   False

c) Temperature is an important factor in the plasticity of fats. Circle the answer.

   True   False

d) Plasticity helps a fat to be spreadable. Circle the answer.

   True   False

4 A student is using the creaming method to make some small cakes.

a) Which **two** ingredients would be creamed together first? [2]

....

b) Checks need to be made during the preparation of the cake mixture. State **one**
characteristic of the creamed mixture to check before flour is added. [1]

....

c) Explain why the mixture would show this characteristic. [2]

....

....

d) How would this help the cakes during baking? [2]

....

....

Review Questions

Raising Agents

1 Explain **four** conditions needed for yeast fermentation.

1 .... [2]

2 .... [2]

3 .... [2]

4 .... [2]

2 A student has been asked to investigate raising agents to make products with light and airy textures.

a) What are raising agents? [3]

....

....

....

b) Complete the table naming **three** differing products the student could make using **three** different raising agents. [6]

Name of Product	Raising Agent Used

3 During food preparation and cooking, physical and mechanical methods are used to help make mixtures light. What equipment or method can be used to assist aeration and lightness when using the following ingredients?

a) Flour for baked goods .... [1]

b) Eggs and caster sugar in a whisked sponge .... [1]

c) What is the main effect of using these methods? .... [1]

Microorganisms, Enzymes and Food Spoilage

1 What is an enzyme? [1]

2 Some fruits and vegetables go brown when they are cut and exposed to oxygen. What is the scientific term for when fruits and vegetables go brown? [1]

3 Name **one** fruit that could turn brown. [1]

4 Suggest **one** method that can be used to slow down the browning process. [1]

Microorganisms in Food Production

1 Tick (✓) **one** answer. Microorganisms are used in the production of: [1]

a) milk, butter and cheese. ☐

b) bread, cheese and yoghurt. ☐

c) salami, sausages and burgers. ☐

d) bread, butter and oil. ☐

2 Which microorganism is used to make salami, pepperoni and chorizo? [1]

3 Yeast is most active at cold and high temperatures. Is this true or false? Tick (✓) **one** answer. [1]

True ☐   False ☐

Practice Questions

Bacterial Contamination

1 Bacterial contamination causes food poisoning. Is this true or false? Tick (✓) one answer. [1]

True ☐   False ☐

2 Which one of the following is important in helping prevent bacterial contamination?
Tick (✓) **one** answer. [1]

a) Clean as you go. ☐

b) Make sure all the kitchen lights are working. ☐

c) Check all equipment is working. ☐

d) Store heavy equipment at a lower level. ☐

3 Explain what the 'use by' date means on a food product. [1]

....

....

Buying and Storing Food

1 Refrigeration is used for food storage to slow down spoilage. Is this true or false?
Tick (✓) **one** answer. [1]

True ☐   False ☐

2 Complete the following sentences using the words in the boxes (continued on page 75).

perishable	1 °C and 4 °C, below 5 °C
cooked	−18 °C and below

a) When preparing food, keep raw and .... foods separate. [1]

b) Chilling high risk/.. foods will slow down the growth of
bacteria. [1]

c) Check the internal temperature of a refrigerator to make sure it is between

.... [1]

d) The temperature of your freezer should be .... [1]

Preparing and Cooking Food

1 Which of the following is most likely to cause cross contamination? Tick (✓) **one** answer. [1]

a) Using ready-to eat-foods within their use-by-date. ☐

b) Placing ready-to-eat foods above raw foods in a fridge. ☐

c) Using the same knife to cut raw chicken and cooked ham. ☐

d) Storing raw chicken in a covered container at the bottom of the fridge. ☐

2 Why should leftover food only be reheated once? [1]

....

....

....

3 Circle the foods that are considered to be high risk. [2]

cooked rice   potatoes   chocolate

tomatoes   cooked chicken   bananas

apples   biscuits

Food Choices

Quick Recall Quiz

You must be able to:

- Understand that religions, customs and beliefs influence food choice
- Know about conditions that may be caused by an intolerance or allergy to food.

Religious Diets

- Some religions have their own dietary laws and rules. For example:
  - Jewish people eat **kosher** food, which means food that has been prepared according to Jewish law.
  - Muslims will only eat meat that is **halal**, where animals are slaughtered in a religiously approved way.

Religion	Dietary Requirements
Judaism	• No shellfish or pork • Only kosher meat • No dairy foods are eaten with meat
Hinduism	• No beef or beef products • Many Hindus are vegetarian
Islam	• No pork • Only halal meat can be eaten
Sikhism	• No beef • Many Sikhs are vegetarian or ovo-lacto vegetarian
Christianity	• No particular dietary restrictions
Buddhism	• Vegetarian
Rastafarianism	• Vegetarian or vegan • White fish sometimes eaten (but no shellfish)

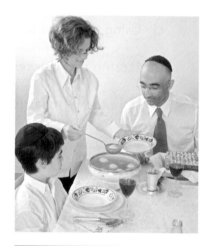

Vegetarians

- Vegetarians don't eat meat, poultry, fish, or products such as gelatin that have been obtained by killing animals.
- Ovo-lacto vegetarians eat eggs and dairy products (but only cheese made with vegetable rennet).
- Lacto vegetarians eat dairy products and honey, but not eggs.
- Vegans do not eat any food with an animal origin. To make sure that their diet is not deficient in certain nutrients (e.g. iron and vitamins D and B12, which are commonly found in animal products), vegans can get the necessary nutrients in their diet from a variety of sources including peas, beans, lentils, nuts and seeds. Soya and fortified products are also sources of protein.
- The reasons why people become vegetarian include: religious dietary laws; ethical reasons, e.g. meat and fish farming being wasteful of the Earth's resources; moral reasons, e.g. animal cruelty; health reasons, e.g. allergies; because they come from a vegetarian family.

> **Key Point**
>
> A diet consists of the foods that a person chooses to eat.

Medical Conditions

- **Diabetes** is a condition caused because the pancreas doesn't produce any, or enough, insulin to control the amount of sugar in the blood.
- **Type 1 diabetes** is often diagnosed in childhood and is not associated with excess body weight. It is treated with insulin injections or using an insulin pump.
- **Type 2 diabetes** is usually diagnosed in over 40-year-olds and is often associated with excess body weight, high blood pressure and/or cholesterol levels at diagnosis.
  - It is treated initially with medication/with tablets. If it cannot be controlled in this way, insulin may have to be injected.
  - 90% of people with diabetes have Type 2 diabetes, which is best treated with a healthy diet and increased physical activity.

Allergies and Intolerances

- **Coeliac** disease is a condition where people have an adverse reaction to gluten, a protein found in wheat, barley, rye, and also oats, which contain a similar substance to gluten.
- Xanthan gum is added to gluten-free flour in order to make the product elastic and stretchy, which can be reduced by the absence of gluten.
- Coeliacs cannot absorb nutrients if they eat gluten. This causes severe pain and can lead to anaemia and **malnutrition**.
- **Lactose intolerance** is caused when the body is unable to digest lactose (a sugar found in milk and dairy products). Lactose intolerance causes stomach upset.
- An **allergy** to nuts can cause **anaphylaxis**, a reaction that can be fatal. People with severe allergies carry an epi-pen in case of an attack.
- Food products must be labelled if they contain nuts, and any of the food allergens specified by the Food Standards Agency must be highlighted on the ingredients list of the product.
- People with a nut allergy have to check that food does not include nuts as an ingredient and that food has been produced in a nut-free environment.

 GLUTEN
 LUPIN
 CELERY
 CRUSTACEANS
 MILK

 SULPHUR DIOXIDE
 SESAME
 MOLLUSCS
 MUSTARD

 TREE NUTS
 EGG
 FISH
 SOYBEANS
 PEANUTS

Products displaying the Crossed Grain symbol have been licensed by Coeliac UK and are safe to eat for those following a gluten-free diet.

Key Words

kosher
halal
vegetarian
ovo-lacto vegetarian
vegan
lacto vegetarian
ethical
diabetes
coeliac
malnutrition
lactose intolerance
allergy
anaphylaxis

Quick Test

1. Which religions traditionally do not eat pork?
2. Which type of vegetarian would not eat honey?
3. Which foods can people with coeliac disease not include in their diet?

British and International Cuisines

You must be able to:

- Understand the meaning of 'cuisine' in terms of the foods related to the traditional eating habits of certain countries
- Learn about the cuisine of two other countries as well as British traditional cuisine.

Traditional British Food

- British food makes use of ingredients produced in the local area.
- British cheeses originate from different parts of the country, e.g. Cheddar (Somerset), Wensleydale (Yorkshire); Red Leicester, Double Gloucester.
- Each cheese has its own distinctive colour, flavour and texture and is made using ingredients from its region of origin.
- There are lots of regional dishes, including Cornish pasties, Lancashire hot pots, Melton Mowbray pies, Eccles cakes, fish and chips and suet-based puddings such as Sussex Pond Pudding.
- Regional dishes normally have historic links. For example, Cornish pasties were eaten by tin miners working underground. The crimped edge was the handle for dirty hands so that the rest of the pastry could be eaten quickly and without mess.

Traditional British meal

Modern British Food

- We now live in a country that is multicultural and people travel to holiday destinations worldwide and are exposed to the cuisines of many other countries. Cheaper air travel prices mean that these countries are more easily accessible to a greater number of people than ever before.
- Supermarkets and specialist shops provide a vast range of ingredients, such as herbs, spices, fruit and vegetables from global cuisines.
- Because of influences from other countries, meals in the UK now contain a wide variety of foods.
- Recipes have been adapted to meet our tastes, e.g. Chicken Tikka Massala (a rich, flavoursome chicken dish without chilli) was invented in the UK but is probably based on Bangladeshi cuisine.

Cornish pasty

Other Cuisines

Spain: Tapas and Paella

- Tapas consist of a wide variety of appetisers or snacks served on small plates and chosen from a menu list.

- Tapas may be cold, e.g. mixed olives or tortilla (a potato omelette) or hot, e.g. chopitos (battered and fried baby squid), garlic prawns (gambas pil pil) and patatas bravas (cubes of potato in a spicy tomato sauce).
- Paella is widely served in restaurants and is traditionally eaten by large groups of people in the street during fiesta times.
- Paella is based on rice from Valencia (a region of Spain) and cooked in a wide flat pan with a mixture of locally sourced foods such as seafood, meat, vegetables and spices, e.g. saffron.

Japan: Fish, Noodles and Rice

- Fish is common in traditional Japanese cuisine as most of the population live near a coastline.
- Other seafoods such as seaweed are also important in the Japanese diet as it is rich in protein and has a flavour that many people love.
- As well as rice, udon noodles are an important ingredient.
- A typical Japanese meal consists of a bowl of rice (**gohan**), a bowl of miso soup (**miso shiru**), pickled vegetables (**tsukemono**) and fish or meat.
- Sashimi consists of thin slices of raw fish pH cooked or other seafood served with spicy Japanese horseradish (**wasabi**) and soy sauce (shoyu).
- Sushi consists of seafood, vegetables and egg served on vinegared rice.

> **Key Point**
>
> 'Cuisine' relates to the established range of dishes and foods of a particular country or region.

> **Key Point**
>
> 'Cuisine' is also concerned with the use of distinctive ingredients and specific cooking and serving techniques.

> **Quick Test**
>
> 1. Name **two** British cheeses that are not mentioned on this spread.
> 2. How well does the traditional British meal match the Eatwell Guide?
> 3. Why does a Cornish pasty have a crimped edge?

> **Key Words**
>
> regional
> multicultural
> cuisine

Sensory Evaluation

You must be able to:

- Understand how to taste food products, using your senses, accurately
- Know about a range of sensory testing methods.

Tasting Food and Drink

- There are five **senses** that are used to **taste** food and drink. A combination of these senses helps you decide if you like a food.
- **Taste**: the tongue can detect five basic tastes: bitter, sweet, salty, umami – a savoury taste, acid/sour
- **Sight**: food's appearance influences how much we want to eat it.
- **Smell**: the **aroma** of food reaches the nose before it reaches the mouth and is tasted.
- **Touch**: what food feels like in the mouth (**texture**).
- **Hearing**: what food sounds like, e.g. sizzling.
- The senses help to develop personal food preferences (likes/dislikes) and evaluate foods, either through preference or discrimination tests.
- A range of accurate sensory words should be used when describing food. These usually come under the headings of: appearance, flavour, texture and aroma.

Basic tastes

Zone of the sour taste
Zone of the bitter taste
Zone of the salty taste
Tip of tongue
Zone of the sweet taste

Controlled Sensory Analysis

- Here are the stages in carrying out a controlled **sensory analysis**:
  - Invite people to be your testers in the sensory analysis.
  - Find a quiet area to work.
  - Give each tester a cup of water to cleanse their **palate** between each sample.
  - Provide small samples of food with clean spoons or forks for each sample. Provide a sheet to record results for each tester.
  - Foods should be identified using codes or symbols so that tasters are not influenced by brand names.
  - Food products should be tested carefully and results recorded accurately.

> **Key Point**
>
> The human **olfactory** system (smell) and taste sensors are important when tasting food.

Paired Preference Tests

- Testers are asked to taste two similar products.
- They are then asked which product they prefer.

Triangle Testing

- Three samples are tested but two are the same.
- The aim is to find out if the tester can pick out which sample is different, e.g. a sauce made with 15% fat or 5% fat. This

Triangle Testing

Which one is the odd one out?

test helps to work out whether a 'healthier' product can be developed without losing taste.

Ranking Tests

- People are asked to taste several products and award scores to decide on the order of preference (best to worst).
- All the samples should be coded.

Rating Tests

- People are asked to say how much they like or dislike a **sensory characteristic** of a product. This is called a **rating**.
- They use a hedonic scale to award a number (using a list provided), or they can indicate which symbol they think is best (most useful for young children).
- Sensory characteristics include sweetness, flavour, colour, texture.

Sensory Characteristic	Testers				Total
	1	2	3	4	
Evenly spread toppings					
Golden brown cheese					
Cheese aroma					
Tomato flavour					
Pizza base texture					
Overall flavour					

KEY
1 = dislike a lot
2 = dislike a little
3 = neither like
    nor dislike
4 = like a little
5 = like a lot

Sensory Profiles

- The results of sensory tests are often displayed visually using charts and sensory profiles, such as the star profile/radar diagram below.

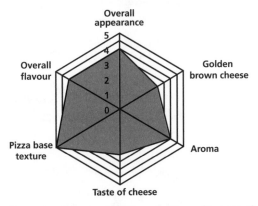

Example: sensory profile for a cheese and tomato pizza.

Quick Test

1. What is another name for the feeling of food in the mouth?
2. Where are the taste sensors in your body?
3. Why is it important to use codes/symbols when tasting foods?

Food Labelling

You must be able to:

- Know which information is legally required for a food label
- Explain how this information will help the consumer
- Understand the ways in which nutritional labelling can be presented.

Food Labels

- The information on a food label is controlled by EU regulations.
- Pre-packaged foods have information labels to inform consumers.
- The following information on food labels is required by law:
  - the name of the food
  - weight or **volume** (indicated by 'e', which stands for 'estimated weight', is normally placed after the total weight of the product in grams – this explains that the weight is estimated and allows for differences)
  - ingredients list (from largest to smallest)
  - **allergen** information
  - GM (genetically modified) ingredients
  - date mark and storage
  - cooking instructions – to ensure food is safe to eat
  - place of **origin**
  - name and address of **manufacturer** (in case of complaint)
  - lot or **batch** mark (for traceability)
  - E numbers – chemical additives that have been approved for use in the European Union
  - nutritional information (from 2016).

Recent Changes to Food Labels

- From December 2016 the rules for **nutrition labelling** in the EU and the FSA in the UK must be followed on **pre-packed** foods.
- The nutrition declaration must include the:
  - energy value in both kilojoules (kJ) and kilocalories
  - amounts in grams (g) of fat, saturates, sugars, protein and salt.
- You must have nutrition labelling if:
  - you make a nutrition or health claim
  - vitamins or minerals are added to the food.

Date Marks and Storage

- **Use by** dates are usually found on high-risk foods. They are safety advice about when the food is likely to be unsafe to eat.
- **Best before** dates are on lower risk foods and indicate when the quality of food may deteriorate.
- **Display until** dates indicate shelf-life in the retail store.
- **Sell by** dates show when the product should be removed from sale to the customer.
- **Storage** dates indicate how the food should be stored in order to maintain freshness and quality.

> ### Key Point
>
> Make sure that you have a good working knowledge of all the information that must be present on a food product label to inform a consumer.

> ### Key Point
>
> EU = European Union
>
> FSA = Food Standards Agency

Serving suggestion
One-sixth of a pack contains

Calories	Sugar	Fat	Satura...
150	**0.4g**	**9.2g**	**4.1g**
8%	<1%	13%	21%...

of your guideline daily amount...

> ### Key Point
>
> You should know the accepted methods of displaying nutritional information on food labels.

The **name** identifies the food. Processed foods must also be identified by the cooking method, e.g. smoked, roast.

Contains GM soya or maize allows consumers to make an ethical choice.

Weight / volume: 'e' indicates approximate weight – allows for tolerances.

Ingredients are listed in **descending order of weight**. The largest amount is first and the smallest amount is the last.

Where a food contains any of the 14 allergens, by law, they must be declared and emphasised in **bold** or colour.

Manufacturer's name or address allows consumers to contact the manufacturer. **Country of origin.**

Shelf life details: the best before date indicates that food is safe to eat but the quality will begin to deteriorate. After the use by date there is a risk of food poisoning. The display by / sell by date tells the retailer what to do with the product.

Instructions for use / heating instructions ensure that the product is cooked at the right temperature and that it's safe to eat.

Storage instructions are shown in words, symbols or temperatures.

The 14 allergens that must be shown on the label are:
- celery
- cereals containing gluten
- crustaceans
- eggs
- fish
- lupin
- cows' milk
- molluscs
- mustard
- nuts
- peanuts
- sesame seeds
- soybeans
- sulphur dioxide (sulphites).

Allergen Information

- There are 14 allergen foods that must be indicated on the label if they are present in the food (see alongside).

Nutrition Labelling Methods

- A front of package label should contain:
  - Information on the energy value in kilojoules (kJ) and kilocalories (kcal) per 100g/ml and in a specified portion of the product.
  - Portion size information expressed in a way that is easily recognisable by, and meaningful to, the consumer.
  - % RI (Reference Intake) information based on the amount of each nutrient and energy value in a portion of the food.
  - Colour coding of the nutrient content of the food. Companies may additionally include the descriptors 'High', 'Medium' or 'Low' (HML) together with the colours red, amber or green respectively to reinforce their meaning.
- **Back of pack** labelling (compulsory in the EU from 2016).
  - The current rules specify the nutrients that can be included.
  - The information has to be presented per 100 g/ml but could also be provided per portion.

Each 1/2 pack serving contains

MED Calories	LOW Sugar	MED Fat	HIGH Sat Fat	MED Salt
353	0.9g	20.3g	10.8g	1.1g
18%	1%	29%	54%	18%

of your guideline daily amount

Key Words

volume
allergen
origin
manufacturer
batch
nutrition labelling
pre-packed

Quick Test

1. When reading a food label, what weight of the food is used?
2. What does EU stand for?
3. What must be included in the nutrition declaration as well as fat, saturates and salt?

Factors Affecting Food Choice

You must be able to:

- Show that you understand that people choose what to eat for a complex variety of reasons
- Provide some reasoned suggestions for food choice based upon occasion, health, lifestyle and income.

Healthy Eating

- The Eatwell Guide is a government guide that advises the public what and how much to eat.
- It makes healthy eating easier to understand by showing a visual image of the types and proportions of foods needed for a well-balanced diet. (see page 28).

Income and Cost of Food

- The income a household has influences food choices.
- Low-income households have to make difficult decisions regarding healthy foods, cost and quality, e.g. protein foods and fresh fruit and vegetables are generally more expensive than starchy foods.
- Where people shop and what they buy is affected by cost.
- Some food retailers market their foods based on high quality and others aim for low cost.
- Increasingly, food banks are used by people on very low incomes.

> **Key Point**
>
> Many factors affect the food choices that people make.

Availability of Food

- There is a vast array of foods to choose from including organic, multicultural and gluten-free.
- The best strategy for a healthy and varied diet is to plan a meal diary for the week, create a shopping list, then look for 'best buys'.

Seasonality

- Seasonal foods are foods that are harvested and consumed in the season they are naturally harvested in.
- In-season foods that are grown and sold locally should have more flavour and nutritional value than imported foods, e.g. English strawberries in June and July.
- Buying locally produced food in season cuts down on food miles and is therefore better for the environment.

Enjoyment of Food

- Our enjoyment of food is affected by what the food looks, smells, tastes and feels like.
- We get maximum enjoyment from eating a variety of textures, flavours and colours.

Lifestyle

- Factors affecting household eating patterns include:
  - work (type of work done/hours worked)
  - travelling time
  - pastimes of individuals
  - the food preparation skills of the individuals in the household unit.
- The amount of time available to prepare and cook food influences:
  - whether to use a microwave oven, a slow-cooker or a conventional oven.
  - the decision to use pre-prepared vegetables or unprepared, fresh vegetables.
  - the type of food cooked, e.g. a casserole or a steak to fry.

Celebrations/Occasions

- Many religious festivals have strong eating traditions, e.g. hot cross buns at Easter, unleavened bread at Jewish Passover.
- Birthday parties or weddings generally include a selection of more expensive and extravagant foods as they are a special time for families.

Marketing Strategies of Retailers

- Marketing strategies are used by retailers to influence the food choices individuals make. These include:
  - special offers
  - in-store promotions
  - advertising
  - recipe cards
  - money-off coupons.

Key Point

People need to make informed choices about the food they buy based on their income, lifestyle and preferences from the food available to them.

Quick Test

1. What does the term 'in season' mean when applied to food?
2. What is the name of the government guide that advises the general public on how much to eat and what to eat?
3. To enjoy eating food, what should our meals contain a variety of?

Key Words

Eatwell Guide
proportions
retailers

Microorganisms, Enzymes and Food Spoilage

1. Bacteria is a microorganism that causes food spoilage. Name **two** other microorganisms that cause food spoilage. [2]

2. State and explain **three** conditions needed for microorganisms to grow. [3]

3. Name **three** foods that spoil easily. [3]

4. Enzymes cause fruit and vegetables to ripen. How does ripening affect fruit? Tick (✓) **one** answer. [1]

   a) They gradually lose their colour. ☐

   b) They start to go brown. ☐

   c) They may go green. ☐

   d) They start to dry out. ☐

Microorganisms in Food Production

1. Microorganisms are used in the manufacturing of certain foods. Explain how they are used in the production of bread. [3]

2 What is used in yoghurt production to develop the taste and texture? [1]

3 Why have probiotic cultures become popular in dairy products? [3]

4 Explain why microorganisms are important in the production of blue-veined cheese. [2]

Bacterial Contamination

1 Bacteria in food can cause food poisoning. Name **two** high-risk foods. [2]

2 There has been an increase of food poisoning in recent years. Describe the main causes of food poisoning. [8]

Review Questions

Buying and Storing Food

1 Complete the following sentences about temperature controls. [4]

a) Water boils at .... °C.

b) The temperature of a freezer should be below .... °C.

c) Bacteria multiply rapidly between .... °C and .... °C.

d) When heating food, the internal temperature should reach .... °C.

2 Tick (✓) the correct box next to each statement to show if it is true or false. [3]

	True	False
a) Lettuce should be stored at the top of the refrigerator.		
b) Hot food should be placed in a refrigerator.		
c) Raw meat should be stored at the bottom of a refrigerator.		

3 Describe **four** ways of reducing the risk of food poisoning when storing food. [4]

....

....

....

....

....

....

....

....

Preparing and Cooking Food

1 Complete the following sentences using the correct temperature. [4]

| 5 °C | 63 °C | 75 °C | 18 °C |

a) Food should be stored in the refrigerator below ....

b) The core temperature of cooked food should reach ....

c) Cooked food should be kept out of the danger zone, which is between

.... and ....

2 What are the recommended temperatures for the following?

Reheating cooked foods: .... [1]

Storing chilled foods: .... [1]

3 Name an item of equipment used to check the temperature of foods when reheating. [1]

....

4 Describe the correct procedures to follow when using the equipment named in question 3. [6]

....

....

....

....

....

....

....

....

Practice Questions

Food Choices

1 Which of the following statements is **true**? Tick (✓) **one** answer. [1]

a) Vegetarians include gelatine in their diet. ☐

b) Kosher meat is eaten by Muslims. ☐

c) Lacto-vegetarians eat honey. ☐

d) Coeliac disease is caused by sensitivity to rice. ☐

2 Underline the correct answer. People with a severe allergy often carry their own medication in the form of… [1]

an epi-pen.   insulin.   a ball-point pen.   Paracetamol.

3 State which nutrients may be missing from a vegan diet. [3]

4 Name **three** protein foods that **each** of the following types of vegetarian may include in their diet.

Vegan: [3]

Lacto: [3]

Ovo-lacto: [3]

British and International Cuisines

1 Which of these cheeses is **not** a British cheese? Tick (✓) **one** answer. [1]

a) Cheddar ☐   b) Brie ☐   c) Wensleydale ☐   d) Stilton ☐

2 Which of these Indian curry dishes was invented in the UK? Tick (✓) **one** answer. [1]

a) Prawn Rogan Josh ☐   b) Chicken Tikka Massala ☐

c) Lamb Khadery ☐   d) Chicken Dopiaza ☐

3 What **four** things make a British cheese distinctive? [4]

4 Add the components of a traditional British meal.

Protein: .... [1]

Starchy food: .... [2]

Vegetables: .... [3]

Sauce: .... [1]

Accompaniment: .... [1]

Sensory Evaluation

1 What is another way of describing 'umami' Tick (✓) **one** answer. [1]

a) A crunchy texture ☐   **b)** A savoury taste ☐

c) An unpleasant smell ☐   **d)** A sour taste ☐

2 Which sense is **least** likely to be needed when evaluating food? Tick (✓) **one** answer. [1]

a) Sight ☐   **b)** Smell ☐   **c)** Hearing ☐   **d)** Touch ☐

3 This is a chart to show the results of testing a pizza.

a) What name is given to this type of chart?

.... [1]

b) Identify the **best** feature of the pizza product tested. [1]

....

c) Identify the two **worst** features (areas to be improved). [2]

....

....

d) What **three** suggestions would you make to improve this product, and why? [6]

....

Food Labelling

1 Which of these items does **not** need to go onto a food label? Tick (✓) **one** answer. [1]

a) Cooking instructions ☐ b) Nutritional information ☐

c) Picture of product ☐ d) Date mark and storage ☐

2 What does 'e' stand for on a product label? Tick (✓) **one** answer. [1]

a) European weight ☐ b) Estimated weight ☐

c) Exceptional weight ☐ d) Extra volume ☐

3 a) Look at the chart below showing the traffic light labelling system.

Per 100g of food			
	Low	Medium	High
Fat	Less than 3g	3g – 20g	More than 20g
Saturated fat	Less than 1.5g	1.5g – 5g	More than 5g
Salt	Less than 0.3g	0.3g – 1.5g	More than 1.5g
Sugars	Less than 5g	5g – 15g	More than 15g

Adapted from the Food Standards Agency

Explain **six** ways in which the traffic light labelling system helps the consumer to make good food choices. [6]

b) Name **three** things that must be included on pre-packed foods. [3]

_____

_____

_____

c) Explain **three** examples of when nutrition information must be provided on a pre-packed food product. [3]

_____

_____

_____

Factors Affecting Food Choice

1 Which of the following food outlets would be used by people on a very low income? Tick (✓) **one** answer. [1]

a) Market stall ☐ **b)** Supermarket ☐

c) Food bank ☐ **d)** Grocer ☐

2 **a)** If you were responsible for feeding young children in your family, what eating model could you use to help you when planning meals? [1]

_____

b) Explain what needs to be considered when planning what to feed a family. Use the following headings and give **two** points for each heading.

What to cook: _____ [2]

_____

How to cook it: _____ [2]

_____

Time: _____ [2]

_____

Food and the Environment

Quick Recall Quiz

You must be able to:

- Demonstrate knowledge and understanding of the environmental issues associated with food and its production.

Food Origins

- Seasonal foods are home-grown products that are traditionally grown or produced during particular seasons of the year, e.g. in the UK strawberries are harvested between June and September.
- Transportation development around the world has meant that when seasonal products are not available they can be imported from hotter climates where they are grown all year round.

Food Miles

- Food miles are the distance food travels from its point of origin to your table.
- The planes, boats and lorries used to transport food around the world all create carbon dioxide gas (CO_2), which is a contributory factor to global warming and climate change (carbon footprint).
- Food miles can be reduced by:
  - supporting British farmers and the economy – use farmers' markets, which showcase local and regional producers
  - eating seasonal products – our bodies get the right delivery of nutrients, minerals and trace elements that we need at the right time of year
  - being a wise shopper – purchase foods that have been produced nearer to Britain.

> **Key Point**
>
> Food and packaging waste contributes to greenhouse gases (GHGs).

Reducing Carbon Emissions

- Recycling and producing less waste also helps to reduce carbon emissions.
- Reducing the amount of packaging or using biodegradable packaging, which rots naturally, could help our environment.
- Recycling (re-using) using local collection facilities or bottle banks is 'green', however some of the chemicals used to clean recycled waste can cause pollution. Recycling may also use more energy than making packaging from new resources.

Food Waste and Landfill

- Nearly a third of all food produced ends up in landfill sites where it gives off methane gas as it decomposes. This gas adds to GHG emissions.

- **Food waste** can be reduced by:
  - using FIFO (First In First Out) storage
  - wise shopping and planning ahead
  - only preparing the food you need
  - using food before it goes out of date
  - using left-over food to make other dishes, e.g. mashed potato can be used to make croquettes for another day.
- Home **composting** is efficient, easy and clean. It benefits the garden and plant life by returning goodness to the soil – just food waste and the earthworms in the ground are needed.

Sustainable Food

- **Sustainable food** means food that will continue to be available for many years to come.
- Intensive farming can diminish the quality of food stocks for future generations.

Fruit and Vegetables

- Follow healthy eating guidelines and eat more fruit, vegetables, grains and pulses, and less animal protein.
- Home-grown garden or allotment fruit and vegetables provide a cost-effective variety of vegetables.

Fish

- Fish can be made more sustainable by:
  - restricting catch sizes
  - imposing minimum sizes of fish for sale
  - widening the selection of fish being eaten to more species
  - putting back young fish so that they can go on to breed and reproduce.
- Dolphin-friendly tuna makes the consumer aware that no dolphins have been accidently trapped in nets during fishing.
- Fishermen have allocated strips of ocean in order to fish sustainably in different areas of the world. There are set fishing regulations and quotas for their area.

Marine Stewardship Council – Seafood can be traced back to a certified sustainable fishery.

> **Key Words**
>
> transportation
> food miles
> climate change
> carbon footprint
> recycling
> packaging
> landfill
> food waste
> composting
> sustainable food

> **Quick Test**
>
> 1. Explain what food miles are.
> 2. How can recycling sometimes produce more pollution than making something from new?
> 3. Give **two** ways that fish stocks can be made more sustainable than intensive fishing.

Food Provenance and Production Methods

You must be able to:

- Demonstrate knowledge and understanding of where ingredients are grown, reared and caught
- Have a clear understanding of different farming methods and their effect on the environment.

Traceability

- **Traceability** means the ability to track any food, feed, food-producing animal or substance that will be used for consumption, through all stages of production, processing and distribution.
- This is so that when a risk is identified it can be traced back to its source in order to swiftly isolate the problem and prevent contaminated products from reaching consumers.

> **Key Point**
>
> Under EU law, all foods need to be traceable from **field to fork**.

Modern Intensive Farming

- After the Second World War, farmers were offered subsidies to farm intensively to produce large-scale, low-cost products.
- This policy has resulted in:
  - fewer small farm communities
  - a greater number of larger business farms
  - large numbers of animals and poultry being kept in massive buildings and fed on high nutrient feeds in a short period of time, which is designed to maximise growth
  - the widespread use of antibiotics, growth enhancers, fertilisers and pesticides
  - small farm fields being opened up – woodland destroyed to make room for large machinery access.
- These methods are also employed all over the world, resulting in large surpluses of food being produced.

Manufacturer
Producer/grower
Distributor
Transportation
Retailer
Consumer

Responsibility for food safety

> **Key Point**
>
> Cheaper foods are ones that are GM/intensively farmed.

Farming Methods

Barn-reared Animals

- **Barn-reared animals** live in an environment similar to intensively-reared animals.
- They have access to natural light from windows.
- They live in a lower density of animals per square metre.
- They have access to environment enrichment such as fresh straw.

Organic Foods

- **Organic** foods are grown naturally without help from any chemical or synthetic treatments.
- They rely on natural compost and manure as fertilisers.
- Organic foods are not **Genetically Modified** – they are GM-free.

- There is no proof that organic food is more nutritious – buying organic food is a lifestyle choice.

Free-range Farming

- **Free-range farming** allows animals or poultry access to outdoor areas for part of their lives.
- Hens that are free-range produce eggs that are more nutritious and tasty. Animals reared this way also have better meat quality.
- Organic and free-range farming are more ethical and have a lower negative environmental impact.

Hydroponic Farming

- **Hydroponic** farming is the production of food using specially developed nutrient-rich liquids rather than soil.
- Hydroponic farming takes place in vast polytunnels or greenhouses in carefully controlled conditions.
- It is an expensive method, so is only used for high-value crops.

Fish Farming

- Increasing demand for fish has seen stocks diminishing in the wild through overfishing.
- The reduction of fish stocks may be due to lack of controls or the use of factory ships that strip the sea of every type of creature.
- **Hatcheries** release young fish into the wild.
- Some **fish farms** are on land, with the fish never exposed to natural resources.
- Fish farm tanks may be giant nets in fresh or seawater, where the fish are controlled, but still in a semi-natural environment.

Genetically Modified (GM) Foods

- This form of **intensive farming** is widely used in agriculture and the food processing industry. It is carefully controlled and regulated.
- GM foods are produced to be more resistant to plant disease, insect pesticides and viruses.
- The DNA in the product can be changed in order for the product to display particular characteristics, e.g. cattle with a higher milk yield, or sheep with a higher meat yield.
- As a result of higher yield, food products are cheaper and harvested in a shorter period of time.
- There are concerns about the use of GM in food production:
    - it is altering and playing with nature
    - possibilities for new strains of microorganisms to develop
    - there are potential risks to long term human (and animal) health and allergic reactions
    - pollen from GM and non-GM crops may potentially be mixed.

> ## Quick Test
>
> 1. Why is it important that the origins of food can be traced?
> 2. What are the benefits of free-range farming?
> 3. Why is hydroponics an expensive farming method?

> ## Revise

> ### Key Point
>
> Best quality protein foods are ones where the welfare of the animals has been considered.

> ### Key Words
>
> traceability
> field to fork
> barn-reared animals
> organic
> Genetically Modified (GM)
> free range farming
> hydroponics
> hatcheries
> fish farms
> intensive farming

Sustainability of Food

Quick Recall Quiz

You must be able to:

- Demonstrate knowledge and understanding of the impact that food has on local and global markets.

Carbon Emissions

- As our Green House Gas (GHG) emissions increase, the planet traps more energy from the Sun.
  - This damages the Earth's ozone layer.
  - This in turn causes changes to climate, and ultimately food and water supplies throughout the world.
- Livestock, especially cows, produce methane gas, which is 20 times more harmful than CO_2.

Global Climate Change Issues

- There are several issues arising from global climate change:
  - Air temperature and rainfall levels rising and falling have an effect on soil. Crops can easily fail as a result.
  - Flooding of areas of land, both coastal and inland.
  - CFCs have depleted the atmosphere's ozone layer and this can have a reduction in yield in some crops with ultraviolet radiation affecting them.
  - Photosynthesis of plants relies on carbon dioxide; increased cloud cover as a result of global warming restricts this from being as efficient.
  - Changes in climate can affect the pests that attack crops, and can change the foods that some helpful bugs use, e.g. bees dying and so not pollinating plants.

Tackling Sustainability of Food Sources

- There are ways that the sustainability of food sources can be addressed:
  - Prevent soil erosion from winds, high rainfall and flooding.
  - Look to improve crop varieties to match climate change, e.g. in drier climates grow crops that require less moisture.
  - Look at crop rotation to reduce soil erosion, and the general health of crops.
  - Put in irrigation systems in drier areas.
  - Increase crop diversity.
  - Improve soil organics by using animal waste.
  - Develop wind breaks.
  - Change the dependence on fossil fuels for transporting foods.

– Tackle deforestation issues – trees remove CO_2 from the atmosphere. Large areas of forest are being cut down in order to graze animals or grow crops. As a result, CO_2 builds up, contributing to global warming, e.g. palm oil producers in Asia have cut down rainforest, which has also affected the habitat of many animals now in danger of extinction.

Sustainable Food

- Sustainable food is food that should be produced, processed, distributed and disposed of in ways that:
  - contribute to thriving local economies and sustainable livelihoods – both in the UK and, in the case of imported products, in producer countries
  - protect the diversity of both plants and animals and the welfare of farmed and wild species
  - avoid damaging or wasting natural resources or contributing to climate change.

Fairtrade

- **Fairtrade** is a foundation that pays a realistic income to farmers in developing countries.
- It ensures a fair price for the goods, giving a steady income, and covers the cost of sustainable production.
- It invests in the locality and in better working conditions.
- Many products now display the Fairtrade mark, e.g. bananas, tea, chocolate and coffee.

Food Assurance Schemes

- Food assurance schemes are guaranteed standards of animal welfare or food safety that the consumer can rely upon.

Red Tractor

- **Red Tractor** is a logo that tells the consumer that the food has been produced, processed and packed to Red Tractor standards.
- The flag on the logo shows the country of origin of the food.
- Red Tractor assures…
  - standards of food hygiene and safety
  - standards of equipment used in production
  - animal health and welfare
  - environmental issues and responsible use of pesticides.
- Red Tractor is controlled and monitored by Assured Food Standards (AFS).
- Any product with this logo can be traced from farm to fork.

Key Point

Sustainable food production ensures less negative impact on the environment and the farmers.

Quick Test

1. What does the flag on the Red Tractor logo mean?
2. How does Fairtrade support farmers in developing countries?
3. Why are large areas of the world being deforested?
4. Which **two** gases contribute to global warming?

Key Words

Green house gas (GHG)
crop rotation
Fairtrade
Red Tractor

Food Production

You must be able to:

- Demonstrate a knowledge and understanding of the primary and secondary stages of food processing
- Demonstrate a knowledge and understanding of the production of two familiar food products.

Milk

- Milk comes from a variety of animals; in Britain we drink mainly cows' milk.
- Fresh milk has a layer of cream on top.
- **Homogenised** milk is forced through tiny holes in a machine. This breaks up the fat and disperses it, and it doesn't reform as a layer.
- Lactose intolerant people can substitute animal milk in their diet with milk made from a variety of sources such as soya, rice, coconut, almond or oat.

Primary Processing

- Using **primary processing**, milk is processed to produce a variety of different types:
  - **Pasteurised** – this extends shelf life.
  - **Skimmed** – this is pasteurised but has had all or most of the fat removed.
  - **Semi-skimmed** – this is pasteurised but has had some of the fat removed.
  - **Ultra-Heat Treated (UHT)** – also known as 'long life', this has a shelf life of up to six months.
  - **Sterilised** – this has a longer shelf life, is homogenised and has a slightly caramel flavour.
  - Dried – does not need refrigeration until reconstituted; it's made by evaporating the water from the milk, which leaves a fine powder; it's non bulky to store.
  - Canned:
    - **evaporated** – milk that has had water evaporated off; it's sweet and concentrated, homogenised and is sealed in cans and sterilised
    - **condensed** – evaporated milk that hasn't been sterilised; it has added sugar and is very thick.

> **Key Point**
>
> Primary processing is the initial process that the food product goes through for us to be able to use it.

Secondary Processing

- **Secondary processing** can be used to process milk into other dairy products:
  - Cream – the fat removed from milk is used. Types of cream are single, whipping, double and extra thick. Cream can be further processed to make soured cream, clotted cream and crème fraiche.
  - Butter – cream is churned to make butter. It can then be salted and made into regional varieties, e.g. ghee, continental.

> **Key Point**
>
> Secondary processing is a further process that can take place using the primary processed product, to make a new food product.

- Cheese – this is milk in its solid form. There are many regional and international varieties of cheese, depending on the methods or animal milks used to produce them.
- Yoghurt – milk has a bacteria culture added to it to make yoghurt. Probiotic products contain live bacteria that are beneficial to the digestive system.
- All dairy products need to be stored in the fridge, except dried and canned milks.

Wheat

- Wheat is the main cereal product. It is used in many countries around the world as it is quite easy to grow and is relatively cheap.
- Each grain of wheat is made up of different layers that have different functions and contain different nutrients.
- Different varieties are grown. Some are stronger than others.

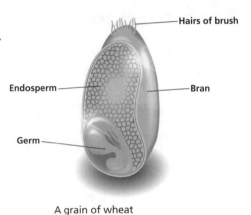

A grain of wheat

Primary Processing

- Wheat can be processed to produce a variety of flours.
- Wheat is made into a flour by a process called **milling**.
  - The grains are blended with other varieties and washed to remove grit and dirt.
  - Huge rotating rollers crush the grains at varying speeds.
  - The crushed grain is sieved and this produces flour.
  - If white flour is wanted, the bran is removed by further rolling.
  - The process is adjusted to produce the required type of flour.

Secondary Processing

- Flour can be further processed to make it into other products such as pasta or bread.
- **Pasta** is made from a variety of strong wheat called durum wheat.
- The flour is further processed by adding it to egg and making a paste, which can then be rolled and shaped to make a variety of pastas.
- **Bread** is made by mixing strong flour (which is high in gluten) with liquid and a raising agent such as yeast.

Key Words

homogenised
primary processing
pasteurised
skimmed
semi-skimmed
Ultra-Heat Treated (UHT)
sterilised
evaporated
condensed
secondary processing
milling

Quick Test

1. What is the outer skin of the wheat grain called?
2. What is homogenised milk?
3. Name **two** types of cream.
4. What type of flour is used to make pasta?

Food Processing

You must be able to:

- Know and understand how processing affects the sensory and nutritional properties of ingredients.

Preservation

- There are four main types of food preservation: high temperature; low temperature; drying; chemical.

High Temperature

Method	Details	Further Information
Canning	• Foods are placed in liquids in cans, sealed and heated to 121 °C • Long shelf life	• Loss of water-soluble vitamins C and B • Change in taste of the food
Irradiation	• Strictly controlled X-rays are passed through the food to delay ripening	• Vitamins A, C, E, and K may be lost • Food looks fresh and tastes the same
Pasteurisation	• Used mainly for milk, heating it to 71 °C for 15 seconds, then rapidly cooling it to 10 °C • Limited shelf life	• Little or no change to taste • Loss of vitamin B2 • Often fortified with vitamin D
Sterilisation	• Heated to 104 °C for 40 minutes or 115 °C for 15 minutes • Used mainly for milk and juices to prolong storage	• The process causes a slight caramelisation of the milk sugar content, resulting in a creamy flavour
Ultra-Heat Treatment (UHT)	• Heated to 140 °C for up to 5 seconds then put in an airtight container • Allows milk to be stored for up to six months	• There is a slight change in taste, colour remains similar and little change in nutrients

- Milk can also be preserved in cans – evaporated milk has water evaporated and is sterilised so it is much thicker and sweeter.
- Condensed milk is not sterilised and has added sugar so it is very sweet and thick.

Low Temperature

Method	Details	Further Information
Freezing	• Food is preserved for up to one year in temperatures between -18 °C and -29 °C	• Generally, no changes to food or nutrient content
Chilling	• This just extends shelf life	
Cold storage (CA)	• This just extends shelf life in an atmosphere of carbon dioxide	

Drying

Method	Details	Further Information
Sunlight	• An old method, which allows moisture to evaporate from the food in the Sun, e.g. fish, meats	• Dehydrating foods can affect colour, e.g. purple plums turn dark brown • They may develop a wrinkly surface/skin • The texture may change as well as the concentration of the flavour • Vitamins C and B6 (and others) may be lost
Oven drying	• Warm ovens are used to dry foods slowly	
Roller drying	• Used for foods that are reconstituted as 'instant' foods, e.g. baby foods	• Loss of vitamins A and C
Spray drying	• This method is used for some foods that are damaged by high heats	
Accelerated Freeze Drying (AFD)	• Food is frozen and the temperature is then increased to make the ice vaporise	• There is no change to the nutrient content of the food and flavour, colour and texture is mostly unaffected

Chemical

Method	Details	Further Information
Vinegar (pickling)	• The strong acid solution preserves the food, e.g. chutney, onions	• Changes to taste, flavour and texture • Shelf life is increased
Sugar	• Fruit is preserved, e.g. jam making	
Salt	• Meat and fish can be salted • Brine solutions can be used to preserve vegetables and canned fish	
Smoking	• Food is 'cooked' by exposing it to heat from wood fires	• Distinctive smoky taste
Alcohol	• Fruits are prepared and stored in brandy	• Changes to taste
Vacuum packaging	• Oxygen is removed from a sealed package, e.g. fish, cheese	• Long shelf life with fresh appearance and taste
Modified Atmospheric Packaging (MAP)	• Sealed packages have oxygen removed and the gas content inside changed, e.g. ready-prepared salads	

Quick Test

1. Which vitamins may be lost during irradiation?
2. What shelf life does UHT milk have?
3. How does vacuum packaging differ from MAP?

Key Words

preservation
temperature
drying
chemical preservation

Review Questions

Food Choices

1 Which religious dietary law forbids shellfish? Tick (✓) **one** answer. [1]

a) Islam ☐   b) Hinduism ☐

c) Sikhism ☐   d) Judaism ☐

2 What condition can be caused if a person has a serious allergy? [1]

3 What is lactose? [1]

4 a) Who is most likely to develop Type 2 diabetes? [2]

b) Explain **two** main recommendations for a diabetic person's diet. [2]

5 What would be the effects of someone suffering from Coeliac disease eating a food containing gluten? [3]

6 What does insulin control in the body? [1]

British and International Cuisines

1 Which country would you associate sashimi with? Tick (✓) **one** answer. [1]

a) China ☐ **b)** Japan ☐ **c)** Spain ☐ **d)** Britain ☐

2 Explain **three** reasons why we now eat foods from other countries in the British diet. Use the following key words to help you.

Multicultural: .... [1]

....

Foods available: .... [1]

....

Lifestyle: .... [1]

....

Sensory Evaluation

1 Which of these statements describes a 'hedonic scale'? Tick (✓) **one** answer. [1]

a) How much someone likes something ☐ **c)** A row of faces ☐

b) How much someone dislikes something ☐ **d)** A list of words ☐

2 Name **three** sensory tasting characteristics. [3]

....

....

3 For each of the following, say which testing method would be the most suitable.

a) To find out which brand of fish fingers is preferred from a range of shops. [1]

....

b) To find out whether people can tell the difference between low-fat cheddar cheese or full-fat cheddar. [1]

4 Explain **two** ways in which the results of sensory testing can be used to develop a food product. [2]

Food Labelling

1 **a)** How much does an average serving of this cereal weigh? [1]

b) How much energy does 100 g of this cereal provide? [1]

c) What could you serve with the cereal to make it healthier? [2]

	100g contains	45g serving contains
...in (19% RDA) and adding a handful of fruit will count as one of your 5-a-Day.		
Typical values		
Energy	1570kJ 375kcal	710kJ 170kcal
Protein	10.3g	4.6g
Carbohydrate	73.8g	33.2g
of which sugars	15.0g	6.8g
Fat	2.0g	0.9g
of which saturates	0.3g	0.1g
Fibre‡‡	8.2g	3.7g
Sodium	0.2g	0.1g
Salt equivalent	0.6g	0.3g

‡‡Fibre has been determined by AOAC analy...
For guideline daily amou...

d) How much of the following nutrients would a serving provide?

Fibre: ....   Saturates: .... [2]

2 Which **four** items on a food label are important for food safety? [4]

3 Which **two** date marks on fresh food tell the customer that the food is safe to eat?
Tick (✓) **two** answers. [2]

a) Sell-by date ☐   **b)** Use by date ☐

c) Display by date ☐   **d)** Best before date ☐

Factors Affecting Food Choice

1 What **four** factors affect our enjoyment of the food we eat? [4]

....

....

2 When feeding a family on a budget, which of the following foods is generally the most expensive to buy? Tick (✓) **one** answer. [1]

a) Chicken ☐   b) Potatoes ☐   c) Frozen peas ☐   d) Bread ☐

3 Explain **two** points about what influences the foods we choose to eat, using the following prompts:

Buying foods in season [2]

....

....

Choosing where to shop [2]

....

....

Cost of food [2]

....

....

Availability of different foods to buy [2]

....

....

4 Which of the following foods are associated with Easter? Tick (✓) **one** answer. [1]

a) Mince pies ☐   b) Hot cross buns ☐

c) Gingerbread ☐   d) Baklava ☐

Practice Questions

Food and the Environment

1 Circle the correct options in the following sentences.

   a) Planes, boats and lorries all create **carbon dioxide / carbon monoxide** emissions. [1]

   b) Food miles are the distance food has travelled from its point of origin to **your supermarket / your table**. [1]

   c) Heavily fertilised crops grown in the UK in heated greenhouses may be responsible for creating **less / more** carbon emissions than imported foods. [1]

   d) FIFO places existing food stock to the **front / back / floor** of food storage areas. [1]

2 What is biodegradable packaging? [2]

   ....

   ....

3 Give **two** benefits of eating seasonal products. [2]

   ....

   ....

4 How can growing fruit and vegetables yourself help the environment? [3]

   ....

   ....

   ....

5 What is seasonality? [1]

   ....

Food Provenance and Production Methods

1 Which of these will help to make the food resource more sustainable? Tick (✓) **one** answer. [1]

   a) Eat more animal proteins. ☐   b) Buy fish that are smaller. ☐

   c) Eat a larger variety of fish species. ☐   d) Eat less fruit and vegetables. ☐

2 How would eating less beef and lamb help the environment? [2]

3 (Circle) the correct answer. [1]

Intensive farming produces food products that are **high cost / low cost**.

4 Name **three** things that are needed by organic farmers so that they can call their products 'organic'. [3]

Sustainability of Food

1 Explain crop rotation. [3]

2 What does GHG stand for? Tick (✓) **one** answer. [1]

a) Good Healthy Goods ☐   **b)** Global Heating Gas ☐

c) Green House Gas ☐   **d)** Genetically Healthier Groups ☐

3 Why is palm oil production damaging the environment? [5]

4 Explain what a Fairtrade product is. [4]

Practice Questions

Food Production

1 What is the difference between fresh milk and homogenised milk? [2]

_____

_____

2 What does UHT stand for? [1]

_____

3 Which type of milk is thicker? Circle the correct answer. [1]

evaporated milk　　　　　　**condensed milk**　　　　　　**sterilised milk**

4 Explain what the term 'primary processing' means. [1]

_____

_____

5 Explain what the term 'secondary processing' means. [1]

_____

_____

Food Processing

1 Name **three** methods of preserving foods using high temperatures. [3]

_____

_____

2 a) Why are some foods irradiated? [1]

_____

b) Name **two** foods that could be irradiated. [2]

_____

3 What does AFD stand for? [1]

....

4 Name **one** benefit of low temperature storage. [1]

....

5 In some hot countries it is traditional to dry foods to preserve them.

a) Explain **one** method of preserving food that is used in a hot country. [1]

....

b) Give **one** example of the method you have chosen. [1]

....

c) Give details of **three** disadvantages of the method you have chosen. [3]

....

....

....

6 a) What does MAP stand for? [1]

....

b) Explain how MAP works. [1]

....

c) Give **two** examples of foods sold in this way. [2]

....

d) Give **three** advantages of using this method. [3]

....

....

....

Review Questions

Food and the Environment

1 Choose the correct words from the boxes and complete the following sentences. [6]

| food waste | green | recycling | energy | pollution | decomposes |

a) Some of the chemicals used to clean during _____ can cause _____.

b) Recycling may use more _____ than making packaging from new resources.

c) _____ can be reduced by wise shopping and planning ahead.

d) Food in landfill sites gives off methane gas as it _____.

e) Recycling is a _____ way of using collection facilities and bottle banks.

2 Explain how the fishing industry can ensure sustainability. [3]

3 What is a landfill? [1]

Food Provenance and Production Methods

1 Choose the correct words from the options given to complete the following sentences. [6]

| GM-free | barn-reared | organic | free-range | intensive farming | lifestyle |

a) _____ produces large-scale, low-cost food in sealed buildings, whereas

_____ animals have access to natural light and some environmental enrichments.

b) _____ grown foods are farmed naturally without any chemical or

synthetic treatments and are _____. This is a _____ choice.

_____ farming allows animals to go outdoors for part of their lives.

2 What is 'traceability'? [5]

....

....

....

3 Is hydroponics an economical way of producing food? [1]

....

4 Name a more economical method of farming with less environmental impact. [1]

....

5 Give **one** disadvantage of the use of factory ships in a fishing fleet. [1]

....

Sustainability of Food

1 Which of these products are Fairtrade products? Tick (✓) the correct answers. [4]

a) Coffee ☐   b) Eggs ☐   c) Chocolate ☐

d) Flour ☐   e) Tea ☐   f) Bananas ☐

2 Products that have a Red Tractor logo on the packaging have a flag also to show the country of origin. [1]

True or **False**? ....

3 What is deforestation? [1]

....

....

4 Name **one** result of deforestation. [1]

....

....

Review Questions

Food Production

1 Is cheese a primary or secondary processed food? .... [1]

2 Name **two** milk products that don't need to be kept in the fridge. [2]

....

3 How is yoghurt made? [1]

....

4 Name **three** different types of cream. [3]

....

5 Name **one** use for:

a) single cream. .... [1]

b) clotted cream. .... [1]

c) crème fraiche. .... [1]

6 Why is cheese difficult to digest? [1]

....

Food Processing

1 Name **two** vitamins that may be lost during the natural sunlight drying process. [2]

....

2 Which of the following are chemical preservation methods? Tick (✓) the correct answers. [2]

a) Spray drying ☐ **b)** Salt ☐

c) AFD ☐ **d)** Smoking ☐

3 Name **one** benefit of low-temperature storage. [1]

....

4 a) Name **three** methods of chemical preservation. [3]

....

....

b) Explain how these methods of preservation are used. [3]

....

....

....

....

....

c) What is the benefit of preserving foods? [1]

....

5 You have been growing your own vegetables and have an excess of tomatoes and onions. How can these be preserved to be used at a later date? Suggest two methods. [2]

....

....

....

6 Name **two** methods that can be used to preserve ham or bacon. [2]

....

....

1. The best method of cooking a quiche is: [1]

   A by steaming. ☐   **B** by grilling. ☐

   C by microwave. ☐   **D** by baking. ☐

2. Circle **one** answer. On a food product label, RI stands for: [1]

   Requires Improvement

   Reference Intake

   Radical Impression

3. Give **three** functions of fat in the diet. [3]

   ....

   ....

   ....

4. When using raising agents, it is important to measure them correctly. Too little raising agent means a lack of rise and gives a close texture. What happens if too much raising agent is measured? [3]

   ....

   ....

   ....

5. When making a sauce it is important to understand heat transfer.

   a) Describe the method of heat transfer from the hob through the saucepan. [1]

   ....

   b) Describe the method of heat transfer through the milk. [1]

   ....

   c) Explain the purpose of stirring (agitating) the milk related to heat transfer. [2]

   ....

   ....

6 Name **two** groups of people who have an increased need for protein in their diets and
   explain why.   [4]

   ....

   ....

7 What particular variety of wheat is used to make pasta flour? Why is this used?   [1]

   ....

8 'Cuisine' relates to: [1]

   A the way in which food is cooked in a kitchen.   ☐

   B the range of dishes and foods relating to a
          particular country or region.   ☐

   C a brand name for kitchen equipment.   ☐

9 Sterilised milk has a long shelf life. Name **three** other types of milk that also have a longer shelf life
   and can be stored prior to use out of the fridge. Explain how each type of milk is packaged.   [6]

   ....

   ....

   ....

10 **a)** Define the term 'coagulation' and describe how it affects the filling of a quiche.   [3]

   ....

   ....

   ....

   b) Give another example of coagulation, apart from in a quiche filling.   [1]

   ....

11 Some ingredients bring about specific characteristics when combined during cooking. Explain
   fully the function of the ingredient used in the following list of food products.

a) Wheat flour in a béchamel sauce. [3]

....

....

b) Rapeseed oil used to roast potatoes. [3]

....

....

c) Egg wash used to glaze pie pastry. [3]

....

....

d) Custard powder used to make vanilla custard. [3]

....

....

12 What are fish farms? Explain how they can help to make fish a more sustainable commodity. [2]

....

....

....

13 A trainee baker needs to recognise characteristics due to caramelisation.

a) Tick the correct examples of caramelisation in the list. [2]

1 Sugars change colour and flavour. ☐

2 Starch turns golden brown. ☐

3 Sugar solution becomes syrup. ☐

4 Enzymic browning on bananas. ☐

b) Explain the problems that would occur if the trainee cooked small sweet buns
for 40 minutes at 210 °C (Gas 7). [3]

_____

_____

_____

14 Which of the following products would show a use-by date? Circle **one** answer. [1]

Packet of dried pasta

Can of soup

Pot of yoghurt

Jar of jam

15 At what temperature should pork be cooked to in order for it to be safe to eat? [1]

A 63 °C ☐   **B** 72 °C ☐

C 74 °C ☐   **D** 78 °C ☐

16 A student is investigating fat and has a list of dishes that contain fat. He needs to identify the main function of fat in each dish. Complete the chart to show the main function of fat within each dish. [5]

Name of Dish	Main Function of Fat in the Dish
a) Pastry pie crust	
b) Hollandaise sauce	
c) Glazed new potatoes	
d) Bread and butter pudding	
e) Steamed syrup sponge	

17 Which **one** of these fish is a white fish? [1]

A Prawn ☐   **B** Mackerel ☐

C Plaice ☐   **D** Scallop ☐

18 Explain intensive animal farming methods. [5]

....

....

....

....

....

....

19 A yeast batter for rich dough needs to be fermented. Describe the conditions needed to enable fermentation to take place. [4]

....

....

....

....

....

20 Which of the following must be included on food labels by law? [3]

A Picture of the product ☐   B Allergen information ☐

C Lot or batch mark ☐   D Ingredients list ☐

21 a) Circle **one** answer. When looking at a traffic light food label, information is given for each food per: [1]

25 g   **100 g**   **200 g**

b) Circle **one** answer. The colours on the traffic light food label help the customer make healthier food choices. The healthiest food choice is shown as: [1]

Red   **Amber**   **Green**

22 What is the term used to describe holding a knife to cut an onion into two on a chopping board? [1]

A Hand ☐   B Bridge ☐   C Claw ☐   D Fist ☐

23 Obesity is considered a major risk to health. Underline **two** medical conditions that are linked to obesity. [2]

dementia   coronary heart disease   lung cancer

conjunctivitis   diabetes   dermatitis

24 When carrying out a tasting panel on a range of similar food products, which of these tests will decide which is the most popular product? [1]

A Rating test ☐   **B** Ranking test ☐

C Triangle test ☐   **D** Paired preference test ☐

25 Are these statements **true** or **false**? Write the answer next to each sentence. [3]

Chopitos consists of cubes of potato in a spicy tomato sauce. ....

Fish is common in traditional Japanese cuisine. ....

A traditional British meal consists of Chicken Tikka Massala with pilau rice. ....

26 Which of these proteins is **not** found in meat? Underline **one** answer. [1]

Elastin

Gluten

Myoglobin

Collagen

27 Identify the conditions that food spoilage organisms need in order to grow. [3]

....

....

....

....

28 Which of the following points should be observed when setting up a tasting session? [2]

A Provide small samples of food. ☐

B Use clean spoons or forks for each sample tested. ☐

C Label foods clearly and accurately. ☐

D Give testers a piece of apple to eat between each sample. ☐

29 Which of the following products is an example of secondary processing? [1]

A Wholemeal flour ☐

B Bread ☐

C Potatoes ☐

D Eggs ☐

30 When filleting a flat fish:

a) What is the first step? .... [1]

b) What type of knife and chopping board would you need? [2]

....

c) Explain **three** points to show how you would know the fish is fresh. [3]

....

....

....

31 Foods that originate in an area of a country generally use locally sourced ingredients. Unravel the following **three** regional British foods. [3]

1 SINROCH TPYAS ....

2 BULDOE ROETSUGELC HSEEEC ....

3 SLECEC SKEAC ....

32 Fruit and vegetables are a good source of dietary fibre. Give **two** reasons why we need plenty of fibre in our diets. [2]

....

....

33 Which part of the body produces insulin? [1]

A Stomach ☐

B Liver ☐

C Pancreas ☐

D Spleen ☐

34 Blue veined cheese is one example of a food where microorganisms are used in food production. Name **one** other food that uses a microorganism in its production process. [1]

....

35 State **three** methods of preserving food at home. [3]

....

....

....

36 Tick the boxes below to show if the statements are **true** or **false**. [3]

Statement	True	False
Vegetarians eat fish		
Hindus eat pork		
Jewish people don't eat shellfish		

37 Fill in the missing word. [1]

Saturated fats raise the c... level in the body.

38 Fillings and dental extractions in children have been linked to overconsumption of which type of carbohydrate? [1]

....

39 Which of the following statements describes the consistency of choux pastry dough? [1]

A Pouring ☐   B Heavy dropping ☐

C Coating ☐   D Soft ☐

40 a) Name **four** of the joints that can be found in a chicken. [4]

....

b) What colour of chopping board should be used to cut chicken? [1]

c) What is the best choice of kitchen knife to use? [1]

d) Explain the process of portioning out a chicken. [5]

41 Which of the following nutrients is **not** found in fish? [1]

A Protein ☐

B Vitamin C ☐

C Zinc ☐

D Omega 3 fatty acid ☐

42 What advice would you give an elderly relative who is planning a healthy diet? [2]

43 Which of the following statements are **true**? [2]

Vegetarians may lack iron in their diet.	
Kosher meat is eaten by Muslims.	
Lacto vegetarians eat honey.	
Coeliac disease is caused by insensitivity to rice.	

44 Name **two** animals and the type of meat produced. [4]

Animal .... Meat ....

Animal .... Meat ....

45 Which of these dough mixtures does **not** use a strong flour? [1]

A Shortcrust pastry ☐   B Pasta ☐

C Choux ☐   D Bread ☐

46 Fruit and vegetables that are produced without the use of artificial fertilisers are called: [1]

A GM (genetically modified). ☐   B sustainable. ☐

C organic. ☐   D intensive farming. ☐

47 What is meant by the term 'food miles'? [1]

....

....

48 Explain the importance of using colour-coded equipment when handling and preparing food. [3]

....

....

....

49 What causes global warming? [1]

....

....

50 Diabetes has increased significantly in the UK over the past few years. [3]

Give **three** types of food you should avoid to decrease your risk of developing this disease.

....

....

51 Complete the chart below. Provide **three** examples of each type of protein. [6]

High Biological Value (HBV) Protein	Low Biological Value (LBV) Protein

Mixed Questions

52 Jake is preparing the following family meal: [8]

Chicken curry with rice

Chocolate mousse

Give Jake advice on how the high-risk ingredients in the meal should be prepared and cooked to avoid food poisoning.

....

....

....

....

....

....

....

....

53 Fill in the missing words. [3]

D... is controlled by careful management of s... in the

diet, plus i... medication.

54 What do the following terms mean? [4]

Enriched bread dough

....

Strong elastic dough

....

Rolling boil

....

A dough

....

55 **a)** What is this logo called? [1]

....

....

b) Where would you be likely to find this logo? [1]

....

c) What does this logo tell you? [8]

....

....

....

....

....

....

....

....

56 Give **two** reasons why someone may need to increase their water intake. [2]

....

....

....

....

57 What is the name given to the production of foods using specially developed nutrient-rich liquids rather than soil? [1]

A Seasonal ☐   **B** Biodegradable ☐

C Hydroponics ☐   **D** Genetically Modified (GM) ☐

Mixed Questions

58 Give **two** functions of vitamin A in the body. [2]

59 Name **three** microorganisms that cause food to spoil. [3]

60 This is a recipe for bread.

200 g strong white flour

1 tablespoon vegetable oil

3 g yeast

3 g salt

150 ml warm water

How could the fibre content of this recipe be increased? [1]

61 Discuss how food poisoning can be prevented when preparing and cooking a chicken stir-fry. [6]

62 Which of these foods is least harmful to the environment? Circle the correct answer. [1]

Roast beef

Lamb stew

Beef burger

Roast chicken

63 Why is white bread a good source of calcium? [1]

....

64 Fill in the missing information. [4]

Method	Details on Main Function of Fat in the Dish
....	Used for foods which are reconstituted as 'instant' foods, e.g. baby foods.
Spray drying	This method is used for some foods that are ....
Accelerated Freeze Drying (AFD)	Food is .... and the temperature is then increased to make the ....

65 Airplanes, lorries and boats are all used to transport food. Which greenhouse gas do they produce? [1]

....

66 Explain what happens to food stored in a refrigerator section where the temperature is 10 °C. [6]

....

....

....

....

....

....

67 Vitamin C is an antioxidant. Which of the following statements best describes the function of an antioxidant? Underline the correct statement. [1]

Antioxidants protect us from pollutants in the environment.

Antioxidants protect us from food poisoning.

Antioxidants protect us from dementia in old age.

68 Look at the refrigerator below and label where the following foods should be stored. [4]

Eggs

Mango

Raw fish

Chocolate eclairs

69 Give **one** function of sodium in the diet. [1]

70 Which vitamin can be manufactured in the body by the action of sunlight on the skin? [1]

71 Vitamin C (ascorbic acid) is water soluble and easily lost in the cooking process.　　　　　[1]

Which of the following is considered good practice to retain the vitamins in vegetable preparation?

A　Prepare vegetables the day before you need them.　☐

B　Put the vegetables in cold water, then bring them to the boil.　☐

C　Cook vegetables very quickly in a small amount of boiling water.　☐

D　Make sure vegetables are very soft before draining and serving.　☐

72 Explain what happens to food stored in a freezer operating at a temperature of −18 °C.　　　[6]

_____

_____

_____

_____

_____

_____

_____

_____

_____

73 Complete the following table.　　　　　[4]

Vitamin	Main Function in the Body	Main Food Sources
Iron		
Calcium		

Total Marks _____ / 212

Answers

Pages 6-15 **Revise Questions**

Page 7 Quick Test
1. With the point facing downwards
2. No
3. To avoid the food moving and the knife slipping
4. Bridge hold; claw grip

Page 9 Quick Test
1. Oily fish
2. **Any two from**: bright eyes, red gills; scales in place; layer of slime; firm flesh; smell of the sea
3. A blue chopping board and a filleting knife

Page 11 Quick Test
1. Covered, in the bottom of the fridge, so that the juices do not drip onto other foods
2. Long fibres
3. Animals; poultry; offal; game

Page 13 Quick Test
1. By hand
2. A mould or your hands
3. Sugar and water

Page 15 Quick Test
1. Strong flour
2. Carbon dioxide
3. To add flavour, colour, and to shorten the dough (restrict gluten development)

Pages 16-19 **Practice Questions**

Knife Skills
1. **c) and d)** **[2]**
2. **Any two from**: Jardinière **[1]** – baton shaped lengths **[1]**; Julienne **[1]** – matchstick-sized strips **[1]**; Macédoine **[1]** – medium-sized dice **[1]**; Chiffonade **[1]** – fine shreds of leafy vegetables **[1]**; Batonnet **[1]** – square-shaped lengths **[1]**; Turning **[1]**, – barrel shaped **[1]**
3. Julienne **[1]**; Batonnet **[1]**; Jardinière **[1]**

Fish
1. **c)** **[1]**
2. **d)** **[1]**
3. a) **Any one of**: Cod **[1]**; Haddock **[1]**; Whiting **[1]**; Pollock **[1]**; Coley **[1]**.
   b) **Any one of**: Plaice **[1]**; Sole **[1]**; Halibut **[1]**; Turbot **[1]**.
   c) **Any one of**: Salmon **[1]**; Sardines **[1]**; Herring **[1]**; Mackerel **[1]**; Tuna **[1]**; Whitebait **[1]**.
4. **Possible responses:** Check that the eyes are bright – dull eyes indicate that the fish may still be safe to eat but is not very fresh **[1]**; Check that the scales are still in place **[1]**; Check that the gills are bright red – if they are dark red, the fish is not fresh **[1]**; Smell the fish – does it have a slightly salty smell of the sea? This is an indicator of freshness, a nasty smell will not improve with cooking **[1]**; Check for a thin layer of clear slime – if the liquid is not clear, the fish has begun to rot **[1]**; Check the flesh is firm with your finger – if the flesh bounces back, it is fresh **[1]**. **(1 mark for each point made, up to a maximum of 5 marks.)**

Meat
1. **b)** **[1]**
2. **d)** **[1]**
3. a) **Any two from**: Stewing **[1]**; Braising **[1]**; Pot roasting **[1]**; Casseroling **[1]**.
   b) Grilling **[1]**; Frying **[1]**
   c) Grilling **[1]**; Frying **[1]**
4.

Temperature check	Time per 500 g
75–80 °C	**30** mins **[1]** + 15 mins
75–80 °C	20 mins + **20** mins **[1]**
Rare: 52 °C Medium: **60 °C [1]** **Well done [1]**: 75–80 °C	20 mins 25 mins 30 mins

5. **Any two from**: Pork **[1]**; Chicken **[1]**; Offal **[1]**. **(Meat products, e.g. sausages, burgers, kebabs, not allowed.)**

Prepare, Combine and Shape
1. **c)** **[1]**
2.

Method	Food
Grating	Cheese **[1]**; Carrot **[1]**
Chopping	Herbs **[1]**; Onion **[1]**
Slicing	**Any two from**: Carrot **[1]**; Onion **[1]**; Bread **[1]**
De-coring	Apple **[1]**; Pineapple **[1]**

Dough
1. **b)** **[1]**
2. **b)** **[1]**
3. Durum wheat **[1]**
4. Glutenin **[1]**; Gliadin **[1]**
5. **Possible responses**: Spinach **[1]**; Beetroot **[1]**; Tomato **[1]**; Squid ink **[1]**; any other suitable answer **[1]**. **(1 mark for each food, up to a maximum of 2 marks.)**
6. Rest it **[1]**; After kneading **[1]**
7. a) Weigh all the ingredients accurately. **[1]**
   b) Add flour immediately to the pan. **[1]**
   c) Add eggs and beat in gradually. **[1]**
   d) Consistency must achieve heavy dropping. **[1]**
   e) Bake in a hot oven. **[1]**

Pages 20-31 **Revise Questions**

Page 21 Quick Test
1. Source of vitamins; Protection for organs; A component of hormones; Energy
2. Amino acids
3. Beans on toast/hummus and pitta bread

Page 23 Quick Test
1. Carbohydrate provides energy
2. Excess carbohydrate is converted to fat and is stored under the skin

3. Non-Starch Polysaccharides (this is dietary fibre)

Page 25 Quick Test
1. Vitamins A, D, E and K
2. **Any three from**: Citrus fruit; Kiwi fruit; Blackcurrants; Tomatoes and green vegetables; Potatoes
3. Folic acid/folate

Page 27 Quick Test
1. To replace supplies lost through blood during periods
2. When bones are at maximum strength
3. Hormones in the thyroid gland
4. **Any two from**: Milk and dairy foods; Green leafy vegetables; Nuts, seeds and lentils; White bread – calcium is added by law; Wholegrain cereals

Page 29 Quick Test
1. **Any three from**: Base your meals on starchy carbohydrates; Eat lots of fruit and vegetables (5–7 portions per day); Eat plenty of fish, including oily fish; Cut down on saturated fat and sugars; Eat less salt – no more than 6g a day for adults; Get active and be a healthy weight; Don't get thirsty (drink 6–8 glasses of water a day); Don't skip breakfast
2. For the development of the neural tube of the foetus
3. The first breast milk, which is full of antibodies
4. Weaning
5. A condition where bones become weak and break easily

Page 31 Quick Test
1. A condition where bones become brittle and break easily
2. Lack of energy; Pale complexion; Shortness of breath; Tiredness.

Pages 32-35 **Review Questions**

Knife Skills
1. Name of knife, **any three from**: Cook's **[1]**; Paring **[1]**; Boning **[1]**; Filleting **[1]**; Carving **[1]**; Bread **[1]**; Palette **[1]**.
   Descriptions **(three from the following, to match the three named)**: Cook's: Comes in different sizes and their strong, ridged blades make them suitable for a wide range of tasks **[1]**; Paring: A small knife with a thin and slightly flexible blade **[1]**; Boning: A very strong blade that will not bend or break easily, can be straight or curved **[1]**; Filleting: Thin-bladed, flexible and very sharp knife **[1]**; Carving: Long blades with a serrated or plain edge, can be rounded or pointed **[1]**; Bread: Long serrated edge **[1]**; Palette: Flexible blade, rounded at the top **[1]**.
   One possible use **(three from the following, to match the three named)**: Cook's, **any one of**: Dicing **[1]**; Chopping and trimming vegetables **[1]**; Chopping and trimming meat and poultry **[1]**; Chopping fresh herbs **[1]**. Paring: Fruit and vegetable

preparation **[1]**. Boning: Removing bones from meat joints and poultry **[1]**. Filleting: Filleting fish **[1]**. Carving: Carving meat joints or cooked hams **[1]**. Bread: Slicing loaves and other bread products, sandwiches **[1]**. Palette, **any one of**: Icing cakes **[1]**; Turning food over during cooking **[1]**; Moulding and smoothing food **[1]**.

Fish
1. d) **[1]**
2. b) **[1]**
3. Method, **any one of**: Canning **[1]**; Freezing **[1]**; Smoking **[1]**; Salting **[1]**. **(1 mark for each method, up to a maximum of 3 marks.)** Canning example, **any one of**: Salmon **[1]**; Tuna **[1]**; Sardine **[1]**; Pilchard **[1]**. Freezing example, **any one of**: Cod **[1]**; Haddock **[1]**; Pollock **[1]**; Coley **[1]**. Smoking example, **any one of**: Salmon **[1]**; Haddock **[1]**; Mackerel **[1]**. Salting example: Cod **[1]**; Herring **[1]**. **(1 mark for each example of method selected, up to a maximum of 3 marks.)**
4. Smoking **[1]**; Salting **[1]**
5. 1 Protein **[1]**; 2 Minerals, **any one of**: iron **[1]**; zinc **[1]**; iodine **[1]**; 3 Vitamins, **any one of**: A **[1]**; D **[1]**; 4 Omega 3 fatty acids **[1]**.

Meat
1. d) **[1]**
2. b) **[1]**
3. a) Pork **[1]**
   b) Beef **[1]**
   c) Lamb/mutton **[1]**
   d) Venison/game meat **[1]**
   e) **Any one of**: Chicken **[1]**; Turkey **[1]**; Duck **[1]**; Goose **[1]**.
4. **Any three from**: Protein **[1]**; Fat (saturated) **[1]**; Iron **[1]**; Calcium **[1]**; Phosphorous **[1]**.
5. **Any three from**: Raw meat should be kept separate from cooked meat to avoid cross-contamination **[2]**; Meat should be stored covered at the bottom of the fridge so that if meat juices leak out they cannot drip onto other foods **[2]**; Chilled meat should be stored at between 0 °C and 5 °C **[2]**; Frozen meat should be stored at between −18 °C and −22 °C **[2]**.

Prepare, Combine and Shape
1. a) **[1]**
2. b) **[1]**
3. b) **[1]**
4. A milk glaze (egg glaze also acceptable) **[1]**
5. **Any two from**: Loaf **[1]**; Cake **[1]**; Jelly **[1]**; Burger **[1]**; Mousse **[1]**.
6. **Any two from**: Consistency in depth **[1]**; Consistency in size **[1]**; Consistency in shape **[1]**.

Dough
1. d) **[1]**
2. a) 1:2 **[1]**
   b) Plain flour **[1]**
   c) Mixture of lard **[1]**; vegetable fat/butter **[1]**
   d) Rubbing-in **[1]**
   e) **Any one of**: short/crisp/light **[1]**
3. a) Acts as a raising agent **[1]**
   b) Feeds the yeast **[1]**
   c) Increases shelf-life/can add colour and flavour **[1]**
   d) Provides the yeast with moisture/helps to form gluten **[1]**

4. It allows the gluten **[1]** in dough to relax **[1]** before it is rolled out.
5. c) **[1]**

Protein and Fat
1. c) **[1]**
2. b) **[1]**
3. Possible answers, **any one of**: Beans on toast **[1]**; Lentil soup with bread **[1]**; Hummus and pitta bread **[1]**; or any other suitable answer **[1]**.
4. b) **[1]**
5. **Any two from**: Full fat milk **[1]**; Hard margarine **[1]**; Coconut oil **[1]**; Palm oil **[1]**; Butter **[1]**; Egg **[1]**; Cheese **[1]**; Cream **[1]**; Cakes **[1]**; Biscuits **[1]**; Chocolate **[1]**; Pastries **[1]**; Meat products **[1]**; Beef fat/dripping/lard **[1]**; or any other suitable answer **[1]**.

Carbohydrate
1. c) **[1]**
2. **Any three from**: Bread **[1]**; Potatoes **[1]**; Pasta **[1]**; Rice **[1]**; Breakfast cereals **[1]**; or any other suitable answer **[1]**.
3. **Any two from**: Carbohydrates are needed by the body because they are the main source of energy in the body for movement **[1]**; Carbohydrates are needed by the body for digestion **[1]**; Carbohydrates are needed by the body for growth **[1]**.
4. Non Starch Polysaccharide **[1]**
5. **Any three from**: Wholegrain cereals **[1]**; Wholemeal bread **[1]**; Wholegrain breakfast cereals, e.g. bran flakes, weetabix, shredded wheat, porridge oats **[1]**; Wholemeal pasta **[1]**; Wholemeal flour **[1]**; Fruit **[1]**; Vegetables **[1]**; Dried fruit **[1]**; Nuts **[1]**; Seeds **[1]**; Beans **[1]**; Peas **[1]**; Lentils **[1]**; or any other suitable answer **[1]**.

Vitamins
1. Vitamin B group **[1]**; Vitamin C **[1]**
2. c) **[1]**
3. **Any four from**: Don't prepare the vegetables too early – the longer fully cooked vegetables sit around before being eaten, the more nutrients are lost **[1]**; Use boiling water when starting off – the vegetables will cook more quickly and more of their nutrients will be retained **[1]**; Use a minimal amount of water to boil vegetables so that any nutrients that leach out are concentrated in a smaller quantity of liquid, that can then be made into a sauce or gravy **[1]**; Do not overcook/leave vegetables al dente, then nutrients won't leach out in the first place **[1]**; Use the cooking liquid to make a sauce/gravy so that any nutrients that have leached into the water during cooking are retained **[1]**; Use a sharp knife and do not over cut – the larger a surface area that can be retained, the more goodness will be locked in **[1]**.
4. Fat-soluble vitamins **[1]**
5. From the action of sunlight on the skin **[1]**; Which enables the body to make vitamin D **[1]**.

Minerals and Water
1. b) **[1]**
2. **Any two from**: Cheese or a named cheese **[1]**; Cream **[1]**; Yoghurt **[1]**; Bread **[1]**; Fish or fish where the bones are eaten **[1]**; Leafy

green vegetables or named vegetable **[1]**; Nuts or named nut **[1]**; Seeds or named seed **[1]**; Dried fruit **[1]**; or any other suitable answer **[1]**.
3. Iron supports the production of haemoglobin in red blood cells **[1]**; Which transports oxygen around the body **[1]**.
4. **Any two from**: Red meat – liver **[1]**; Lentils **[1]**; Dried apricots **[1]**; Cocoa **[1]**; Chocolate **[1]**; Corned beef **[1]**; Curry spices **[1]**; Green leafy vegetables **[1]**; Fortified breakfast cereals **[1]**; or any other suitable answer **[1]**.
5. **Any three from**: Water is essential for normal brain function **[1]**; Drinking enough water decreases the risk of kidney problems **[1]**; Drinking the right amount of water helps to maintain normal blood pressure **[1]**; Water aids bowel movements **[1]**; Water helps to maintain cell function/healthy skin **[1]**; The right amount of water in the body regulates temperature **[1]**; Water is needed to maintain hydration **[1]**; Water aids digestion **[1]**; Water is needed to make body fluids, e.g. blood, saliva and mucus membranes **[1]**.

Making Informed Choices
1. Eatwell Guide **[1]**
2. **Any three from**: Eat less sugar **[1]**; Eat more fibre **[1]**; Eat more starchy food **[1]**; Eat at least five portions of fruit and vegetables daily **[1]**; Don't skip breakfast **[1]**; Eat the right amount to stay a healthy weight **[1]**; Follow the Eatwell Guide **[1]**; Drink plenty of water **[1]**.
3. Weaning **[1]**
4. Carbohydrates **[1]**

Diet, Nutrition and Health
1. b) **[1]**
2. b) **[1]**
3. **Any two from**: Coronary heart disease **[1]**; Type 2 Diabetes **[1]**; Some types of cancer **[1]**; High blood pressure **[1]**; Risk of stroke **[1]**; Arthritis **[1]**; Breathing problems **[1]**.
4. Insulin **[1]**
5. **Any three from**: Weight gain/obesity **[1]**; Can produce high/bad cholesterol **[1]**; Can block arteries **[1]**; Angina **[1]**; Coronary Heart Disease (CHD)/heart disease/heart attack **[1]**; Trans fats/higher risk of cancer **[1]**.
6. BMR is the body's basic energy rate if the person is at complete rest **[1]**; BMR is the energy needed by the body just to function, with no movement except breathing/natural functions at rest **[1]**.

Page 41 Quick Test
1. True
2. Convection
3. Water-based; Fat-based; Dry
4. Conduction; Convection; Radiation

Page 43 Quick Test
1. Enzymes
2. Coagulation/Denaturation

Page 45 Quick Test
1. Gelatinisation
2. Radiation/grill
3. True

Page 47 Quick Test
1. Shortening
2. True
3. Creaming

Page 49 Quick Test
1. Air is the raising agent
2. Air expands when heated
3. By forming a foam
4. By turning to steam

Pages 50-53 **Review Questions**

Protein and Fat
1. chicken [1]; milk [1]; soya [1]
2. Protein complementation [1]
3. The level of cholesterol [1]

Carbohydrate
1. pasta [1]; potato [1]; oats [1]
2. lentils [1]; cabbage [1]; apples [1]; shredded wheat [1]
3. Sugar [1]

Vitamins
1. Kiwi fruit [1]; lemons [1]; cabbage [1]
2. Folate (folic acid) reduces the risk of neural tube defect (Spina Bifida) in babies, so pregnant women should take a folate (folic acid) supplement [1].
3. **Any two from**: Vitamin C and vitamin B are destroyed by heat so vegetables that are not subjected to heat retain these vitamins [1]; Vitamin C is destroyed on exposure to oxygen therefore after it has been cut, before cooking, there are losses [1]; Vitamin C and vitamin B are water-soluble so will leach into water during the cooking process [1]
4. Ascorbic acid [1]

Minerals and Water
1. haemoglobin [1]; red blood [1]; oxygen [1]
2. Due to monthly menstrual blood loss [1]
3. The body's metabolic rate [1]
4. **Any two from**: In hot weather to replace water lost by excess sweating [1]; After physical exertion to replace water lost by excess sweating [1]; Lactating mothers need an increased supply of water for the production of milk [1]; People suffering from sickness and diarrhoea need to increase their intake of water in order to keep hydrated due to loss of water via the sickness and diarrhoea [1].

Making Informed Choices
1. chocolate [1]; beef [1]; apricots [1]
2. c) [1]
3. iron [1]; liver [1]

Diet, Nutrition and Health
1. a) [1]
2. milky drinks [1]; cheese [1]; yoghurts [1]
3. Diabetes is controlled by careful management of sugar in the diet [1]; In addition, insulin medication may be frequently injected [1].
4. c) [1]
5. In old age bones become weak and brittle and are more likely to break – this is when the condition of osteoporosis is most likely to occur [1].

Pages 54-57 **Practice Questions**

Cooking of Food, Heat Transfer and Selecting Appropriate Cooking Methods
1. a) microorganisms [1]
   b) shelf life [1]; keep quality [1]
   c) variety [1]
   d) digest [1]
2. Conduction [1]; Convection [1]; Radiation [1]
3. Water-based methods, **any two from**: Boiling [1]; Stewing [1]; Steaming [1]; Poaching [1]; Braising [1]; Pressure cooking [1].
   Dry cooking methods, **any two from**: Baking [1]; Grilling, [1]; Roasting [1]; Barbecuing [1]; Dry-frying [1].
   Fat-based **any two from**: Shallow frying in fat [1]; Deep-fat frying [1]; Stir frying, etc. [1].

Proteins and Enzymic Browning
1. Heat [1]; Reduction of pH [1]; Enzymes [1]; Mechanical actions [1]
2. a) It changes from being runny to being set [1]
   b) Due to coagulation [1]; Due to the effect of heat [1]
3. a) Gluten [1]
   b) Strong flour contains more protein than soft cake flour [1].
4. a) Water must be added [1]; Kneading must take place [1]
   b) Gliadin [1]
5. a) Enzymic browning [1]
   b) **Any one of**: Inactivate enzymes by using an acid such as lemon juice [1]; Remove the presence of air, e.g. place in water [1]; Cook [1].

Carbohydrates
1. liquid [1]; gelatinisation [1]; heated [1]; stirred [1]; boiling point [1]
2. a) Colour: The bread turns golden [1] Flavour: The bread tastes sweeter [1] Texture: The bread becomes crisp [1]
   b) Dextrinisation [1]
   c) Hygroscopic [1]
   d) The toast becomes less crisp [1]

Fats and Oils
1. a) [1]
2. a) Functions: Aerate mixture [1]; Trap air [1]; Characteristics: Cake rises [1]; Increased volume [1]
   b) Function: Shorten the dough [1]; Characteristic: Crumbly short texture [1]

Raising Agents
1. To increase volume [1]; To make a light texture [1]; To raise mixtures [1]
2. a) Air [1]
   b) The raising agent is incorporated by whisking air into the sponge mixture, either by hand or with an electric mixer [1]
   c) **Any one of**: Baking powder [1]; Bicarbonate of soda [1]; Cream of tartar [1].
   d) Carbon dioxide [1]
   e) During baking the heat of the oven causes the raising agents to be active and produce the gas [1]; The gas swells with heat and raises the scone [1].

Pages 58-67 **Revise Questions**

Page 59 Quick Test
1. Bacteria
2. Between 5 °C and 63 °C – this is known as the 'danger zone'
3. Eat food as soon as possible after making/cooking, if not cool down as quickly as possible and store in the fridge or freezer
4. Possible answers: Bread; Wine; Beer

Page 61 Quick Test
1. Lactobacillus
2. Mould
3. Safeguard the immune system; Improve digestion; Keep the body's intestine balanced

Page 63 Quick Test
1. Any or all of the following are possible: Stomach pains; Diarrhoea; Vomiting; Nausea (feeling sick); Fever
2. **Any three from**: Salmonella; Staphylococcus Aureus; Clostridium perfingens; Clostridium Botulinum; Bacillus cereus; E-Coli; Listeria; Campylobacter; Norovirus
3. Raw food; Bacteria passed on from people; Bacteria carried in air and dust; Bacteria on equipment and utensils; Soil; Pests; Contaminated water; Degrading food waste
4. Very young children and babies; Elderly people; People who have a serious illness or are recovering from a serious illness; Pregnant women and nursing mothers; People who have allergies

Page 65 Quick Test
1. The 'Use by' and 'Best before' dates
2. Between 1 °C and 4 °C to make sure that food is held below 5 °C
3. False
4. −18 °C or below
5. Ice crystals remain at the centre; Cooking will melt the ice but the correct core temperature may not be achieved and bacteria may survive

Page 67 Quick Test
1. **Any four from**: Before preparing food; Between handling raw and high-risk or ready-to-eat foods; After you have been to the toilet; After sneezing or coughing; After changing a waterproof plaster; After using cleaning fluids; After handling food waste or rubbish; After handling known allergens
2. The thickest part of the food (core) should reach 75 °C, or 70 °C for two minutes

Pages 68-72 **Review Questions**

Cooking of Food, Heat Transfer and Selecting Appropriate Cooking Methods
1. In the following order: flavours [1]; mouthfeel/texture [1]; texture/mouthfeel [1]; bulk [1]; colour [1].
2. Conduction occurs as heat transfers through the pan [1]; This heat comes from the heat source [1]; Convection takes place in water in a pan during boiling [1]; Heat passes through the potato by conduction [1]; Boiling uses two methods of heat

transfer, the first method is conduction [1]; The second method is convection [1].

Proteins and Enzymic Browning
1. Meaning: Protein denaturation means the functional properties [1]; of a protein change [1].
   Example, possible answer: An example is cooked egg white [1]; It is denatured and therefore it will not whip to a foam [1].
2. In the following order: gluten [1]; elastic [1]; kneading [1]; short [1]; structure [1]

Carbohydrates
1. The solution becomes viscous when water and sugar are heated together [1]; The colour of this liquid becomes increasingly golden [1]
2. Flour: Dextrinisation [1]
   Sugar: Caramelisation [1]
3. Dextrinisation, possible answers, **any one of**: Brulee [1]; Crème caramel [1]; Spun sugar [1]; Sweet making [1]; Sticky ribs or wings [1] or any other suitable answer [1]. Caramelisation, possible answers, **any one of**: Toast [1]; Au gratin [1] or any other suitable answer [1].
4. a) Choice: Recipe B [1]
   b) Explanation: The amount of flour would thicken the milk [1]; To make a smooth coating sauce [1]; The amount of flour in Recipe A would not be enough [1]; the sauce would remain runny [1].

Fats and Oils
1. a) The rubbing-in method [1]
   b) Fat coats the flour grains – the fingertips are used [1]; Added water does not penetrate the flour grains [1]; Therefore, gluten [1] development is limited [1]; Pastry not kneaded [1]. Cooking denatures the gluten and the pastry texture is crumbly, crisp and short [1].
2. In the following order: Emulsions [1]; immiscible [1]; separates [1]; stable [1]; lecithin [1]; natural [1]
3. a) True
   b) False
   c) True
   d) True
4. a) The margarine/butter [1]; and the caster/baking sugar [1]
   b) The mixture becomes paler as the fat and sugar are creamed together [1]
   c) Trapping air (aeration) [1]; Causes a paler coloured air-in-fat foam to form [1]
   d) During baking the trapped air would expand [1]; This makes the cakes rise [1]

Raising Agents
1. 1 A warm temperature is needed [1]; Of 25 °C–35 °C [1]
   2 Moisture is needed [1]; This is supplied from the liquid in the recipe [1]
   3 The yeast requires food [1]; This is supplied by the flour or the added sugar [1]
   4 Time is needed [1]; To produce the gas that raises the mixture [1]
2. a) Raising agents are active ingredients that make food products rise or processes that make food products rise [1]; and have open airy textures [1];

Raising agents can be biological, chemical or mechanical (physical) [1]
   b) Name of product, possible answers, **any three from**: Scones [1]; Yeasted products [1]; Choux pastry [1]; Batters [1]; Whisked sponge [1] or any other suitable answer [1]. **[The correct raising agent must then be matched to each product to gain the mark.]**
   Name of raising agent, **any three from**: Scones: baking powder/bicarbonate of soda [1]; Yeasted products: yeast [1]; Choux pastry: high moisture content provides steam during the baking process that raises the mixture [1]; Batters: air whipped in during mixing process/baking powder/bicarbonate of soda/cream of tartar [1]; Whisked sponge: air whisked in during mixing process [1].
3. a) A sieve can be used to pass air through the flour [1].
   b) Whisking, by hand or with and electric mixer, distributes air through the mixture [1]
   c) Both of these methods add air [1]

Microorganisms, Enzymes and Food Spoilage
1. Enzymes are molecules that control chemical reactions in food [1]
2. Enzymic browning [1]
3. Apple/banana [1]
4. **Any one of**: Coat the fruit in an acid such as lemon/lime juice [1]; Coat the fruit in sugar to halt/prevent browning [1]; Stop oxygen from turning the fruit brown by immersing the fruit in water or juice [1]

Microorganisms in Food Production
1. b) [1]
2. Lactic acid [1]
3. False [1]

Bacterial Contamination
1. True [1]
2. a) [1]
3. It means that the food is safe to eat up until the date marked on the food product or its packaging [1]

Buying and Storing Food
1. True [1]
2. a) cooked [1]
   b) perishable [1]
   c) 0 °C and 4 °C, below 5 °C [1]
   d) −18 °C and below [1]

Preparing and Cooking Food
1. c) [1]
2. If food is not reheated properly, the bacteria in it may survive and multiply – every time food is reheated the chances of this happening are increased [1]
3. cooked rice [1]; cooked chicken [1]

Page 77 Quick Test
1. Judaism and Islam
2. A vegan does not eat honey

3. Foods that contain gluten, e.g. wheat, barley, rye

Page 79 Quick Test
1. Possible answers: Cornish Blue (from Cornwall), Lanark Blue (from Scotland), Caerphilly (from Wales)
2. Roast meat, beans, pulses and fish all provide protein. Roast potatoes (starchy carbohydrate) and accompanying vegetables provide at least two of the five recommended portions of vegetables per day.
3. The crimped edge of a Cornish pasty provided a 'baked-in' handle for tin miners to hold while they ate the pasty.

Page 81 Quick Test
1. Texture
2. On your tongue
3. So that the tester is not influenced by brand loyalty

Page 83 Quick Test
1. 100 g
2. European Union
3. The following must also be included: Kilocalories and kilojoules; Protein; Sugars

Page 85 Quick Test
1. Foods that are harvested and consumed in the season they are naturally harvested in.
2. The Eatwell Guide
3. A variety of textures, flavours and colours

Microorganisms, Enzymes and Food Spoilage
1. **Any two from**: Yeast [1]; Mould [1]; Fungi/fungus [1].
2. **Any three from**: The length of time exposed – the longer the exposure, the greater the growth [1]; Temperature – the higher the temperature, the faster and greater the growth [1]; Moisture – the higher the level of moisture the greater the growth [1]; The amount of microorganisms originating in the food itself influence growth – the more microorganisms there are to begin with, the more rapid their growth [1]; Level of oxygen/air/air flow – the more exposure to oxygen, the greater the chance of growth [1]; Neutral pH [1].
3. **Any three from**: Milk/yoghurt [1]; Meat/poultry [1]; Fish/shellfish [1]; Eggs [1]; Vegetables [1]; Salad [1]; Fruit [1]; Bread [1]; Cream [1]; or any other suitable answer [1].
4. b) [1]

Microorganisms in Food Production
1. **Any three from**: Bread dough is mixed and kneaded, millions of air bubbles are trapped and distributed through the dough [1]; The yeast in the dough provides microorganisms, which absorb the starches and sugars in the flour, turning them into alcohol and carbon dioxide gas [1]; This gas expands the air bubbles, causing the bread to rise [1]; During rising, the yeast divides and multiplies, producing more carbon dioxide. As long as there is ample air and food (carbohydrates) in the dough, the yeast will multiply until its activity is stopped by the heat of the oven [1].

2. A culture is used to develop taste and texture [1].

3. Probiotic cultures offer health benefits such as helping to improve digestion [1]; Safeguarding the immune system [1]; Keeping the body's intestinal flora in balance [1].

4. The cheese is treated with mould, which contains microorganisms, and these microorganisms develop as the cheese matures [1]; The mould continues to develop throughout the process, imparting the blue-veined appearance of the cheese and giving flavour [1].

Bacterial Contamination

1. Any two from: Poultry – chicken/duck/turkey/goose [1]; Meat – beef/lamb/pork/sausages/burger [1]; Offal – liver/kidneys [1]; Fish/shellfish [1]; Eggs [1]; Dairy Products – cream/milk/yoghurt [1]; Cooked rice **(no marks awarded for 'rice' only)**/reheated rice [1]; Custards/sauces/gravy [1]; Credit will also be given for a named food product, e.g. chicken curry containing fresh cream [1].

2. Any eight from: The presence of excess microorganisms in food are a major cause of food poisoning – usually bacteria but sometimes viruses [1]; Food that has not been cooked properly, e.g. eggs that are still raw/undercooked products, i.e. meats [1]; Food that has not been stored properly, e.g. where cross contamination has taken place between raw and cooked meats [1]; Food poisoning takes place when microorganisms are allowed to multiply at a high rate, this is when they produce toxins/poisons/waste products (microorganisms cause the symptoms of food poisoning) [1]; A lack of knowledge and understanding about how to store, cook and prepare foods in the home and or in industry can lead to food poisoning [1]; Intensive farming methods can lead to disease spreading easily in perishable foods such as poultry or seafood, thus leading to food poisoning [1]; Dirty water can be a cause of food poisoning as the water can carry bacteria into the body [1]; Pests/animals can transmit food poisoning via bacteria/pests [1]; Poor standards of food hygiene in people handling food can transmit food poisoning to themselves and to others [1]; Dust and soil can carry food poisoning onto or into food [1]

Buying and Storing Food

1. a) Water boils at **100 °C**. [1]
b) The temperature of a freezer should be below **–18 °C**. [1]
c) Bacteria multiply rapidly between **5 °C** and **63 °C**. [1]
d) When heating food, the internal temperature should reach **75 °C**. [1]

2. a) False [1]
b) False [1]
c) True [1]

3. Any four from: Ensure the food is cooled before refrigerating or freezing it as the microorganisms will continue to multiply. If the food is hot, then it heats the fridge or freezer and therefore puts all the food within the danger zone [1]; Ensure the food is kept in the refrigerator (between 0 and 5 °C) so that it is out of the 'danger

zone' where microorganisms are most active [1]; Cool food quickly as this limits microorganism growth time, ensuring less time in the 'danger zone' [1]; Do not leave food out for long periods of time as this encourages the growth of microorganisms [1]; Keep food out of the 'danger zone' of 5–63 °C because this is where the microorganisms are most active – out of this range the microorganisms remain inactivated [1]; Use the food within a few days of cooking/opening because exposure to air and temperatures once open encourages food to deteriorate and microorganisms to multiply [1]; Transfer food to containers from tins and cans because open cans encourage microorganism activity and can lead to poisoning from the can oxidising [1].

Preparing and Cooking Food

1. a) 5 °C [1]
b) 75 °C [1]
c) 5 °C [1]; 63 °C [1]

2. Reheating cooked foods: 75 °C (**accept 72 °C–75 °C**) [1]
Storing chilled foods: blast chilling 4 °C is within range (**accept** 0–4 °C **or** 'below 5 °C') [1]

3. A food or temperature probe [1] (**'thermometer' will not be accepted**)

4. Sterilise/clean with antibacterial wipe (**clean not acceptable unless qualified, 'disinfect' will not be accepted**)/make sure sterile before and after use [1]; Check reading before start (ideally room temp), do not touch container/baking tin with probe, then place into centre of food/core temperature [1]; Keep in place for two minutes [1]; Check temperature is 75 °C or over [1]; Remove from food/take the reading when it is stable/after two minutes [1]; If not at correct temperature continue cooking food and check temperature again later [1].

Pages 90-93 **Practice Questions**

Food Choices

1. c) [1]
2. an epi-pen [1]
3. Iron [1]; vitamin D [1]; Vitamin B12 [1]
4. Vegan, **any three from**: Peas (any type) [1]; Beans (any type) [1]; Lentils (any type) [1]; Nuts (any type) [1]; Seeds (any type) [1]; Soya products [1].
Lacto: Milk [1]; Cheese [1]; + any vegan food [1].
Ovo-lacto: **any three from**: Eggs [1]; Milk [1]; Cheese [1]; Quorn [1] + any vegan food [1]

British and International Cuisines

1. b) [1]
2. b) [1]
3. Own colour [1]; Own texture [1]; Own flavour [1]; Ingredients from the region that produces the cheese [1]
4. Protein: Any choice of meat (or vegetarian equivalent) [1]
Starchy food: Roast or creamed potatoes [1]; Yorkshire pudding [1]

Vegetables, **any three from**: Carrots [1]; Broccoli [1]; Peas [1]; Any other suitable vegetable [1]
Sauce: Gravy [1]
Accompaniment, **any one of**: Mint (with lamb) [1]; Apple (with pork) [1]; Horseradish (with beef) [1]

Sensory Evaluation

1. b) [1]
2. c) [1]
3. a) Star profile/Radar diagram [1]
b) Pizza base texture [1]
c) Taste of cheese [1]; Golden brown cheese [1]
d) Use stronger cheese [1]; to improve the taste of the pizza [1]
More cheese when cooked [1]; would improve both colour and flavour [1]
Cook pizza for longer [1]; until the cheese browns in the oven [1].

Food Labelling

1. c) [1]
2. b) [1]
3. a) Any six from: Traffic light labelling educates consumers so that they can make informed choices [1]; Traffic light labelling identifies the nutritional content levels of the food [1]; Traffic light labelling is easy to read/interpret [1]; Colours may be explained: Red = poor choice for healthy eating [1]; Amber = caution in quantities eaten [1]; Green = free to eat in high quantities [1]; Should aim for more green, less red, and moderate amounts of amber foods [1].
b) Any three from: Energy value in kilojoules [1]; Energy value in kilocalories [1]; Amount in grams of fat [1]; Amount in grams of saturates [1]; Amount in grams of sugars [1]; Amount in grams of protein [1]; Amount in grams of salt [1].
c) Any three from: When the supplier makes a nutrition claim for the food product [1]; When the supplier makes a health claim for the food product [1]; If vitamins are added to the food product [1]; If minerals are added to the food product [1]

Factors Affecting Food Choice

1. c) [1]
2. a) The Eatwell Guide [1]
b) What to cook, **any two from**: What do people in the family like? [1]; What ingredients are needed? [1]; How many people are you catering for? [1]
How to cook it, **any two from**: Equipment available [1]; Skill needed [1]; Recipe [1]
Time, **any two from**: When the food has to be served [1]; Who is eating and when [1]; How long you have to cook the food [1]

Pages 94-103 **Revise Questions**

Page 95 Quick Test

1. Food miles are the distance that food travels from its origin to your plate

2. Recycling can use more energy to produce new packaging and some solutions used to clean recycled products are polluting

3. **Any two from**: Restrict catch sizes; Have minimum sizes of fish allowed to be kept for sale; Widen the selection of fish being eaten to more species; Put caught young fish back in the sea so that they can go on to breed and reproduce.

Page 97 Quick Test

1. So that if a risk is identified, the source can be quickly isolated and consumers can be protected

2. Animals have access to the outdoors as they would in nature; They can behave and feed naturally; The resulting product is better quality as the animal has not suffered stress

3. Hydroponic farming requires large areas of glasshouses, with controlled systems where the products grow in nutrient-rich liquids, without soil

Page 99 Quick Test

1. The Red Tractor logo flag shows the country of origin of the food product

2. Fairtrade products give a realistic income to the farmer; Fair prices for the goods; Local investment; Better working conditions

3. To make way for growing crops and animal grazing

4. Methane and CO_2

Page 101 Quick Test

1. Bran

2. Milk that has been processed to distribute the fat content throughout

3. **Any two from**: Single; Whipping; Double; Extra thick; Crème fraiche; Soured; Clotted

4. Durum wheat flour

Page 103 Quick Test

1. Vitamins A, C, E, and K

2. Six months

3. Vacuum has oxygen removed and MAP has oxygen removed and replaced with another gas

Pages 104-107 **Review Questions**

Food Choices

1. d)   **[1]**
2. Anaphylaxis (or Anaphylactic shock)   **[1]**
3. Lactose is a sugar   **[1]**
4. a) People over 40 **[1]**; People who are overweight **[1]**
   b) Healthy diet **[1]**; Increased physical activity **[1]**
5. The sufferer would experience severe stomach pain **[1]**; The sufferer would experience anaemia **[1]**; The sufferer would eventually experience malnutrition **[1]**
6. Blood sugar level   **[1]**

British and International Cuisines

1. b)   **[1]**
2. Multicultural: due to the influence of people originally from other countries (or previous generations of their families) now living in the UK **[1]**
   Foods available, **any one of**: Specialist food shops that cater to particular cuisines or ethnic groups increase the diversity of food available **[1]**; International foods are now

available to buy online and in supermarkets **[1]**; Recipe books that explain how to make food from all over the world are readily available and relatively cheap to buy from bookshops or online **[1]**; Free recipes from all over the world are available online **[1]**. Lifestyle, **any one of**: People now routinely take holidays to other countries, where they are exposed to different cuisines – they may take the new ingredients and recipes home with them **[1]**; We have a diverse range of takeaways/restaurants that sell the cuisines of other countries **[1]**.

Sensory Evaluation

1. a)   **[1]**
2. **Any three from**: Sweetness **[1]**; Flavour **[1]**; Colour **[1]**; Texture **[1]**; Appearance **[1]**.
3. a) Ranking test   **[1]**
   b) Triangle test   **[1]**
4. So that the best aspects of the product can be retained **[1]**; So that the worst aspects of the product can be changed **[1]**.

Food Labelling

1. a) 45 g   **[1]**
   b) 1570 kJ/375 kcal   **[1]**
   c) Handful/portion **[1]**; of fruit **[1]**
   d) Fibre: 3.7 g **[1]**; Saturates: 0.1 g **[1]**
2. **Any four from**: Allergen information **[1]**; Date mark **[1]**; Cooking instructions **[1]**; Storage instructions **[1]**; Batch mark **[1]**.
3. b) **[1]**; d) **[1]**

Factors Affecting Food Choice

1. What the food looks like **[1]**; What the food smells like **[1]**; What the food tastes like **[1]**; What the food feels like in the mouth **[1]**
2. a)   **[1]**
3. Buying foods in season: In-season food has more flavour **[1]**; In-season food has more nutritional value **[1]**
   Choosing where to shop, **any two from**: Type of shops available **[1]**; Income available **[1]**; Access – transport **[1]**
   Cost of food, **any two from**: What income is available **[1]**; Quality v cost **[1]**; Cost of seasonal food **[1]**; Taking advantage of special offers **[1]**
   Availability of different foods to buy, **any two from**: Multi-cultural influences **[1]**; Organic food choices **[1]**; Gluten-free options **[1]**
4. b)   **[1]**

Pages 108-111 **Practice Questions**

Food and the Environment

1. a) carbon dioxide   **[1]**
   b) your table   **[1]**
   c) more   **[1]**
   d) front   **[1]**
2. Packaging that rots naturally **[1]**; Packaging that rots quickly **[1]**.
3. The body gets delivery of the correct nutrients for that time of year **[1]**; also trace elements and minerals for the correct time of year **[1]**.
4. You only pick what you need for that meal so there is less waste **[1]**; You have a variety of seasonal foods at the right time of year for your body's needs **[1]**; It is cost-efficient **[1]**.

5. The peak harvest time for crops in the UK/the time of year when there is most demand for a particular crop   **[1]**

Food Provenance and Production Methods

1. c)   **[1]**
2. Less methane being produced by animals **[1]**; More land available to grow high-protein crops, e.g. soya **[1]**.
3. low cost   **[1]**
4. **Any three from**: Grown naturally **[1]**; No chemical or synthetic treatments **[1]**; No antibiotics **[1]**; Natural manure and compost only as fertilisers **[1]**; Must be GM-free **[1]**.

Sustainability of Food

1. Growing different crops **[1]**; in a field each year to reduce soil erosion **[1]**; and improve general health of crops **[1]**.
2. c)   **[1]**
3. Rainforest **[1]**; has been cut down **[1]**; to grow and harvest palm trees on the land **[1]**. The trees in the rainforest remove CO_2 from the atmosphere **[1]**. Also, the rainforest is the habitat of many animals now facing extinction **[1]**.
4. **Any four from**: Farmers in developing countries get realistic incomes **[1]**; Investment in local community **[1]**; Better working conditions **[1]**; Fair price for goods **[1]**; Sustainable production **[1]**.

Food Production

1. Fresh milk has cream on top **[1]**; Homogenised has the cream dispersed throughout the milk **[1]**.
2. Ultra Heat Treated
3. condensed milk
4. The changing or converting of raw food materials into, e.g. food that can be eaten immediately or be processed into other food products (wheat into flour) **[1]**.
5. The changing or conversion of primary processed foods into other food products, which may involve combining one or more food ingredients, e.g. flour into pasta **[1]**.

Food Processing

1. **Any three from**: Canning **[1]**; Irradiation **[1]**; Pasteurisation **[1]**; Sterilisation **[1]**; Ultra heat treatment **[1]**.
2. a) Foods are irradiated to delay ripening.**[1]**
   b) Any two fruits or vegetables named that are imported from other countries, e.g. strawberries, bananas **[2]**.
3. Accelerated Freeze Drying   **[1]**
4. Generally there is no change to the food or nutrient content **[1]**.
5. a) Sunlight drying, which allows moisture to evaporate from the food in the sunshine   **[1]**.
   b) **Any one of**: Fish, e.g. cod **[1]**; Meat, e.g. beef jerky **[1]**; Fruit, e.g. grapes– raisins **[1]**.
   c) **Any three from**: Can affect the natural colour **[1]**; May develop a wrinkly surface **[1]**; Texture change **[1]**; Loss of vitamin C and B6, as well as others **[1]**.
6. a) Modified Atmospheric Packaging **[1]**
   b) Sealed packages have oxygen removed and the gas content inside changed **[1]**.

c) **Any two from**: Ready-prepared salads [**1**]; Vegetables [**1**]; Fruits [**1**].

d) Longer shelf life [**1**]; Fresh appearance [**1**]; Fresh taste [**1**].

Food and the Environment

1. a) Some of the chemicals used to clean during **recycling** [**1**] can cause **pollution** [**1**].

   b) Recycling may use more **energy** [**1**] than making packaging from new resources.

   c) **Food waste** [**1**] can be reduced by wise shopping and planning ahead.

   d) Food in landfill sites gives off methane gas as it **decomposes** [**1**].

   e) Recycling is a **green** [**1**] way of using collection facilities and bottle banks.

2. Restriction on the sizes of catches allowed [**1**]; Ensuring that fish caught must be returned if they don't meet a minimum size requirement [**1**]; Encouraging the public to eat a wider variety of fish [**1**].

3. A site where rubbish is dumped and buried [**1**].

Food Provenance and Production Methods

1. a) **Intensive farming** [**1**] produces large-scale, low-cost food in sealed buildings, whereas **barn-reared** [**1**] animals have access to natural light and some environmental enrichments.

   b) **Organic** [**1**] grown foods are farmed naturally without any chemical or synthetic treatments and are **GM-free** [**1**]. This is a **lifestyle** [**1**] choice. **Free-range** [**1**] farming allows animals to go outdoors for part of their lives.

2. The ability to track any food [**1**]; animal feed [**1**]; food-producing animal [**1**]; or substance [**1**]; that will be used for consumption through all stages of production, processing and distribution [**1**].

3. No, it is very expensive [**1**]

4. Organic/free range [**1**]

5. They strip the seabed bare of every living creature for miles [**1**].

Sustainability of Food

1. a) c) e) f) [**4**]

2. True [**1**]

3. Large areas of forest being cut down in order to graze animals or grow crops [**1**].

4. **Any one of**: CO_2 builds up, which contributes to global warming [**1**]; Animals lose their natural habitat, putting them in danger [**1**]; Deforested land suffers from soil erosion and becomes infertile [**1**].

Food Production

1. Secondary [**1**]

2. Canned milk [**1**]; Dried mik [**1**].

3. Bacteria culture is added to milk. [**1**]

4. **Any three from**: Single [**1**]; Double cream [**1**]; Extra thick [**1**]; Soured [**1**]; Clotted [**1**]; Crème fraiche [**1**].

5. a) **Any one of**: Pouring over desserts [**1**]; Sauces [**1**].

   b) **Any one of**: Serving with ice cream [**1**]; Scones (clotted cream tea) [**1**].

   c) In place of cream in recipes (as it has a lower fat content) [**1**].

6. During processing the protein content of the milk coagulates and shrinks [**1**].

Food Processing

1. Vitamin B6 [**1**]; Vitamin C [**1**]

2. b) d) [**2**]

3. Usually no change to food or nutrient content [**1**].

4. a) **Any three from**: Vinegar [**1**]; Sugar [**1**]; Salt-brine solution [**1**]; Smoking [**1**]; Alcohol [**1**]; Vacuum packing [**1**]; MAP [**1**].

   b) **Any three from**: Vinegar – in pickling [**1**]; Sugar – in jam-making [**1**]; Salt-brine solution – for fish and meat [**1**]; Smoking – food cooked by heat from wood fires [**1**]; Alcohol – fruit stored in brandy [**1**]; Vacuum packing – oxygen is removed from the sealed package [**1**]; MAP – sealed package has gas content inside changed [**1**].

   c) All preserving methods are used to prolong shelf life [**1**].

5. Pickled in vinegar to make, for example, chutney/pickled onions/tomato sauce [**1**]; Both could also be chopped and frozen [**1**].

6. **Any two from**: Smoking [**1**]; Vacuum packaging [**1**]; Salt [**1**].

1. D [**1**]

2. Reference intake [**1**]

3. **Any three from**: Used for energy [**1**]; Helps insulate the body/keep warm [**1**]; Provides the body with fat-soluble vitamins A, D, E and K [**1**]; A component of hormones [**1**].

4. **Any three from**: a coarse texture results [**1**]; Over-rise takes place [**1**]; Collapse/sink in product's structure [**1**]; Unpleasant taste [**1**].

5. a) Heat is transferred from the hob through the saucepan by conduction [**1**].

   b) Heat is transferred through the milk by convection [**1**].

   c) Stirring (agitating) the milk distributes the heat throughout the milk [**1**]; preventing lumps [**1**].

6. **Any two from**: Babies/children [**1**] for growth [**1**]; Adolescents [**1**] for growth spurts [**1**]; Pregnant women [**1**] for the growing baby [**1**]; Nursing mothers [**1**] for lactation (milk production) [**1**].

7. Durum wheat; Stronger [**1**] [**both answers needed for 1 mark**]

8. B [**1**]

9. **Any three from**: Condensed milk [**1**] in tins [**1**]; Evaporated milk [**1**] in tins [**1**]; Dried milk [**1**] in card containers [**1**]; UHT milk [**1**] in card cartons [**1**].

10. a) Coagulation is the denaturation of protein [**1**]; It can be caused by heat during cooking [**1**]; It makes a quiche filling set [**1**].

    b) **Any one** example of cooked egg: Cakes [**1**]; Puddings [**1**]; Omelette [**1**].

11. a) Wheat flour thickens [**1**]; gelatinises [**1**]; during the cooking [**1**]; of the milk-based sauce.

    b) Rapeseed oil makes the potato starch [**1**]; turn golden brown [**1**]; during high temperature roasting [**1**].

    c) Egg wash makes the pastry golden and shiny [**1**]; as the proteins (coagulate) [**1**]; during baking [**1**].

    d) Custard powder is cornflour, vanilla and yellow colour – so it thickens [**1**]; flavours [**1**]; and colours [**1**]; the milk.

12. They may be tanks on land or nets floating in seawater or fresh water [**1**]; Fish stocks are controlled, but still within a semi-natural environment [**1**].

13. a) 1 and 3 must be ticked. [**1**]

    b) Charred/blackened/burnt buns would indicate a colour change [**1**]; Charred/blackened/burnt buns would give a bitter taste [**1**]; Overbaked buns would be hard and unpleasant to eat [**1**].

14. Pot of yoghurt [**1**]

15. D [**1**]

16. a) Shortening [**1**]
    b) Emulsification [**1**]
    c) Gloss/flavour [**1**]
    d) Enriching [**1**]
    e) Aerating [**1**]

17. C [**1**]

18. **Any five from**: Large farms [**1**]; Large numbers of animals in crowded buildings [**1**]; Massive buildings [**1**]; No access to natural resources for the animals, e.g. daylight [**1**]; Very few farm workers needed to run computerised feeding systems [**1**]; Antibiotics used on the animals [**1**]; Growth enhancers used on the animals [**1**].

19. Conditions required are: Food – from sugar or flour [**1**]; Time – to allow doubling of dough size [**1**]; Moisture – the liquid in the recipe [**1**]; Warmth – 20–25 °C [**1**].

20. B [**1**]; C [**1**]; D [**1**]

21. a) 100 g [**1**]
    b) Green [**1**]

22. B [**1**]

23. Coronary Heart Disease [**1**]; Diabetes [**1**]

24. B [**1**]

25. In the following order: False [**1**]; True [**1**]; False [**1**]

26. Gluten [**1**]

27. **Any three from**: Warm temperature/37 °C [**1**]; Moisture [**1**]; Food [**1**]; Time [**1**]; Neutral pH [**1**]; May need oxygen [**1**].

28. A [**1**]; B [**1**]

29. B [**1**]

30. a) Remove the head [**1**]

    b) Filleting/Cook's knife [**1**]; Blue board [**1**]

    c) **Any three from**: Eyes are bright and not dull [**1**]; Scales are in place [**1**]; Gills are bright red [**1**]; Slightly salty smell of the sea [**1**]; Thin layer of slime [**1**]; Flesh is firm [**1**].

31. 1 Cornish pasty [**1**]; 2 Double Gloucester cheese [**1**]; 3 Eccles cakes [**1**]

32. **Any two from**: To make food passing through digestive system soft and bulky [**1**]; Helps prevent constipation [**1**]; Helps prevent diverticular disease and some forms of cancer [**1**].

33. C [**1**]

34. **Any one of**: Bread/or named bread [**1**]; Yoghurt/or named yoghurt [**1**].

35. **Any three from**: Making jams/jellies/crystallising [**1**]; Pickling/chutneys [**1**]; Bottling [**1**]; Drying [**1**]; Freezing [**1**]; Salting [**1**]; Smoking [**1**].

36. Vegetarians eat fish: False **[1]**; Hindus eat pork: False **[1]**; Jewish people don't eat shellfish: True **[1]**
37. cholesterol **[1]**
38. Sugar **[1]**
39. B **[1]**
40. a) **Any four from**: Breast **[1]**; Leg **[1]**; Wing **[1]**; Drumstick **[1]**; Thigh **[1]**
    b) Red **[1]**
    c) Boning knife/Cook's knife **[1]**
    d) Remove legs **[1]**; Separate the drumstick and the thigh **[1]**; Remove wings **[1]**; Find the wishbone at the front of the bird, release the wishbone **[1]**; cut through the knuckle at the base, then carefully remove the breasts from the carcass **[1]**.
41. B **[1]**
42. **Any two from**: Follow the Eatwell Guide **[1]**; Eat smaller portions **[1]**; Drink plenty of water **[1]**; Make sure that your diet contains plenty of calcium-rich foods to help prevent osteoporosis **[1]**.
43. True statements: Vegetarians may lack iron in their diet **[1]**; Lacto vegetarians eat honey **[1]**.
44. **Any two from**: Pigs – pork **[2]**; Cattle – beef **[2]**; Sheep – lamb **[2]**; Deer – vension **[2]**.
45. A **[1]**
46. C **[1]**
47. Food miles are the distance food travels from where it is produced to where it is eaten (also known as 'field to fork') **[1]**.
48. **Any three from**: To avoid cross contamination **[1]**; To keep raw foods and cooked foods apart **[1]**; To avoid bacteria transfer **[1]**; Reference to named bacteria **[1 mark per bacteria, up to three bacteria]**; Examples – chopping boards/knives/storage containers can be colour coded **[1]**; Colours used to identify equipment – Raw meat – red/Salad and fruit – green/Fish – blue/Vegetables – brown/Cooked meat – yellow/Bakery and dairy – white **[1]**.
49. Global warming is caused by CO_2 emissions trapping the Sun's energy **[1]**.
50. **Any three from**: Table sugar (sucrose) **[1]**; Honey **[1]**; Jam **[1]**; Fruit juice **[1]**; Sweets **[1]**; Chocolate **[1]**; Cakes **[1]**; Biscuits **[1]**; Sugary drinks **[1]**.
51. High biological value (HBV) protein, **any three from**: Meat **[1]**; Fish **[1]**; Eggs **[1]**; Cheese **[1]**; Milk **[1]**; Soya **[1]**.
    Low biological value (LBV) protein, **any three from**: Nuts **[1]**; Seeds **[1]**; Lentils **[1]**; Pulse vegetables **[1]**; Bread **[1]**.
52. **Any eight from**: Identification of chicken as a high-risk ingredient **[1]**; Identification of eggs as a high-risk ingredient **[1]**; Identification of cream as a high-risk ingredient **[1]**; Identification of rice as a high-risk ingredient **[1]**; Cross contamination should be avoided **[1]**; Correct storage temperatures should be observed **[1]**; Food hygiene and cleaning procedures must be applied to hands, hair, etc. and equipment **[1]**; Correct reheating temperatures must be observed **[1]**; Correct cooking temperatures must be achieved **[1]**; Storage after cooking should meet the correct standards **[1]**.

53. Diabetes **[1]**; sugar **[1]**; insulin **[1]**
54. Enriched bread dough: the addition of sugar, butter and maybe egg **[1]**.
    Strong elastic dough: stretchy dough that does not break and shrinks back when pulled out of shape **[1]**.
    Rolling boil: Water that has been heated to the point where it has large bubbles that break on the surface **[1]**.
    A dough: A mixture that contains flour, and possibly other ingredients, held together by a liquid **[1]**.
55. a) The Red Tractor logo (controlled and monitored by Assured Food Standards (AFS)) **[1]**
    b) On food labels or on food packaging **[1]**
    c) **Any eight from**: The Red Tractor logo tells us that the food has been produced **[1]**, processed **[1]** and packed **[1]** to Red Tractor standards; The flag on the logo shows the country of origin **[1]**; The logo assures high standards of food hygiene and safety **[1]**; The logo assures high standards of equipment used in production **[1]**; The logo assures high standards of animal health and welfare **[1]**; The logo assures high standards in environmental issues and the responsible use of pesticides **[1]**; Any product with this logo can be traced from farm to fork **[1]**.
56. **Any two from**: In hot weather to replace water lost by excess sweating **[1]**; After physical exertion to replace water lost due to excess sweating **[1]**; Lactating mothers need an increased supply of water for the production of milk **[1]**; People suffering from sickness and diarrhoea need to increase their intake of water due to water loss through sweating/vomiting/excess excretion **[1]**.
57. C **[1]**
58. **Any two from**: Maintenance of normal iron metabolism **[1]**; Maintenance of normal vision **[1]**; Maintenance of skin and the mucus membranes **[1]**.
59. Moulds **[1]**; Yeast **[1]**; Bacteria **[1]**
60. **Any one of**: Use wholemeal or granary flour **[1]**; Use seeds as a topping **[1]**.
61. **Any six from**: Check the ingredients are fresh/within their sell-by date **[1]**; Do not use the same equipment to cut up the raw chicken and the vegetables **[1]**; Wash your hands before and after handling the raw chicken **[1]**; Use colour-coded equipment to avoid cross contamination **[1]**; Use the correct storage temperatures **[1]**; Ensure that the chicken is refrigerated until just before use **[1]**; Wash the chopping boards before use **[1]**; Follow food hygiene and cleaning procedures **[1]**; Use the correct reheating temperatures **[1]**; Use the correct cooking temperatures **[1]**; Make sure that the core temperature of the chicken reaches 70–72 °C (piping hot) **[1]**; Check that the chicken is cooked, e.g. cut it to check that the meat is not pink inside **[1]**; Cook the chicken prior to adding the vegetables **[1]**; Follow the correct storage procedures after cooking (cool quickly, cover properly, store in a fridge) **[1]**.

62. Roast chicken **[1]**
63. Calcium is added to white bread by law (fortified) **[1]**
64. Method: Roller drying **[1]**
    Details, spray drying: This method is used for some foods that are damaged by dry heats **[1]**.
    Details, AFD: Food is frozen **[1]** and the temperature is then increased to make the ice vaporise **[1]**.
65. Carbon dioxide **[1]**
66. **1–2 marks from**: Refrigerator temperature of 10 °C is too high/incorrect **[1]**; This temperature is in the danger zone/5–63 °C **[1]**
    Any further 4 marks from: Effects on food stored at 10 °C: Perishable food will have its shelf life reduced/food will not last as long **[1]**; Bacteria will grow/breed **[1]**; Chilled food will not be safe to eat **[1]**; Danger of food poisoning **[1]**; Health concerns if food is eaten **[1]**; Quality of food will suffer, e.g. texture **[1]**; Correct temperatures should be: 1–60 °C for perishables **[1]**; Correct temperature range for high-risk perishables is 1–4 °C **[1]**.
67. Antioxidants protect us from pollutants in the environment **[1]**.
68. Eggs – in the door **[1]**; Mango – in the salad drawer **[1]**; Raw fish – on the bottom shelf or below the chocolate éclairs **[1]** **[the raw fish must be below the chocolate éclairs, fish in the salad drawer will not be accepted]**; Chocolate eclairs – on the first shelf or second shelf **[1]** **[must be above the raw fish]**.
69. **Any one of**: Sodium regulates the amount of water in the body **[1]**; Sodium assists the body in the use of energy **[1]**; Sodium helps to control muscles and nerves **[1]**.
70. Vitamin D **[1]**
71. C **[1]**
72. **Any six from**: Water in food/stored here remains frozen/solid **[1]**; Fast freezing produces small ice crystals so reduces damage to food structure **[1]**; Sensory properties, e.g. taste, flavour, colour, shape are maintained for most foods (not some fruit/veg) **[1]**; Nutritional value is maintained **[1]**; Food does not decay while correct temperature and storage time are maintained **[1]**; Shelf life of food is extended **[1]**; Bacteria stop growing – become dormant – water changes to ice crystals, making it unavailable for bacterial growth **[1]**; Bacteria not killed – will become active again on thawing **[1]**; Enzyme action is slowed down but not destroyed **[1]**.
73. Iron, main function in the body: Manufacture of haemoglobin in red blood cells **[1]**.
    Iron, main food sources: Red meat, especially liver **[1]**.
    Calcium, main function in the body: Strengthening of bones and teeth **[1]**.
    Calcium, main food sources: Milk and dairy products **[1]**.

Glossary

A

aeration processes in food preparation that incorporate air to give light, open textures or assist rising

allergy conditions, such as itchy skin or restricted breathing, caused by sensitivity to something in the environment or to a food

allergen a food that causes a bad chemical reaction

amino acids small molecules that form long chains in proteins

anaemia if there is a deficiency of iron in the blood, it is called anaemia; symptoms include tiredness

anaphylaxis an acute allergic reaction to a food, e.g. nuts, that can, in extreme cases, lead to death

antioxidants these help to protect cell membranes and to maintain healthy skin and eyes; vitamin E is an antioxidant

aroma a distinctive (usually pleasant) smell of a food

ascorbic acid another name for vitamin C

B

bacteria single-celled organisms that are able to reproduce rapidly (also called microorganisms); bacteria are sometimes useful and are used to help make food, e.g. cheese, and are sometimes harmful (pathogenic) and can cause food poisoning

barn-reared animals animals bred and housed in a large barn, rather than fully outdoors or in cages

Basal Metabolic Rate (BMR) the energy needed by the body to power your internal organs when completely at rest

batch the quantity of food products made in one operation, e.g. scones, bread rolls

batonnet ingredients cut into square-shaped lengths

best-before date a safety date found on foods and their packaging; best-before dates usually appear on foods that have a long shelf life such as canned, dried and frozen food products

binding various ingredients, such as water, egg, flour or breadcrumbs, are used to 'bind' other ingredients together

Biological raising agent using yeast, a microscopic plant that ferments, to produce carbon dioxide

Body Mass Index (BMI) a measure that adults can use to see if they are a healthy weight for their height; the ideal healthy BMI is between 18.5 and 25

bridge hold a knife skill technique where the food being cut is secured with one hand held in the shape of a bridge, while the free hand slices beneath 'the bridge' with the knife

C

caramelisation change of colour and flavour when heating sugar or a sugar solution

carbon dioxide gas (CO_2) gas produced from yeast and chemical raising agents

carbon footprint the total amount of greenhouse gas emissions something causes – the 'something' can be an individual, a country, an event, a journey, etc.

cardiovascular anything that relates to the heart and blood vessels

chemical preservation any chemical that is added to a food product in order to extend its shelf life; chemical preservation usually inhibits the growth of bacteria

chemical raising agents food-safe chemicals that produce carbon dioxide gas, e.g. bicarbonate of soda, baking powder

chiffonade the name given to the technique of cutting leafy green vegetables into fine shreds

chilled food food that must be stored at a temperature of below 5°C

cholesterol a type of fat found in the blood, which is made in the liver and is also obtained from the food you eat; there is 'good' cholesterol (called HDL, high-density lipoprotein) that helps to break down fat and 'bad' cholesterol (called LDL, low-density lipoprotein) that clogs up blood vessels

chopping to cut something up using a knife

choux a type of pastry used for eclairs, choux buns and gougères

claw grip a knife skill technique where the food being cut is secured with one hand held in the shape of a claw, while the free hand slices the food with the knife

climate change a change in global or regional temperatures caused by increased levels of carbon dioxide due to the intensive use of fossil fuels such as coal and oil

coagulate protein denaturation by heat

coating a covering of one type of food product by another, e.g. fish coated in breadcrumbs

cobalamin another name for vitamin B12

coeliac coeliac disease is caused by the body's immune system mistaking substances in gluten (a protein found in wheat, barley, rye, and also oats, which contain a similar substance to gluten), as a threat and attacking them; Coeliacs cannot absorb nutrients if they eat gluten – this causes severe pain and can lead to anaemia and malnutrition

collagen the name of the main structural protein in connective tissue

colostrum the first milk produced by a lactating mother; it is full of antibodies that are useful to the new-born baby

combining to mix ingredients together, either by hand or with a machine such as a hand mixer

composting to make a compost out of decayed plant matter that can be used to fertilise new plants

condensed a liquid such as milk that has been evaporated, has not been sterilised, and has had sugar added to it

conduction heat transfer from one molecule to another

connective tissue tissues made of fibres that form a framework in the body to bind or separate other tissues and organs

constipation when faeces become difficult to expel from the body because they are hard and small

consistency mouthfeel sensory term related to thickness and smoothness of a mixture

contamination when a food product has become impure via contact with a harmful material, e.g. bacteria

convection heat transfer by rising and falling currents in a liquid or air

cooking the application of heat to change food from raw to cooked

core temperature the temperature at the centre of cooked food; reheated food should reach a core temperature of 75°C

creaming beating together yellow fat and caster sugar to aerate it

crop rotation the practice of growing different crops every year in the same field – switching the type of crop grown helps to keep the soil fertile

cross-contamination transferring bacteria from one place to another

crustacean crabs, lobsters, prawns, crayfish, shrimp and squid are all crustaceans

cuisine a style or method of cooking characteristic of a particular country, region or establishment

D

danger zone 5°C–63°C; the temperature zone that food must be kept out of because it is the zone in which bacteria will multiply and contaminate foods

dehydration the process of the removal of water

denaturation changing protein function by heat (cooking), acids, or mechanical actions

dextrinisation browning due to dry heat, charring food

diabetes   a medical condition caused by the inability of the pancreas to produce any, or enough, insulin to control the amount of sugar in the blood

dicing   to cut food into cubes

dietary fibre   a type of carbohydrate; it cannot be digested to provide energy

disaccharides   complex sugars that are formed when two monosaccharides join together

diverticular disease   when pouches form in the intestines that then become infected with bacteria

drying   to remove most or all of the moisture from a food; usually done to extend the shelf life of the food

E

Eatwell Guide   a guide that shows the proportions in which different groups of foods are needed in order to have a well-balanced and healthy diet

elastin   a protein found in connective tissue that functions together with collagen; elastin can recoil like a spring and is found in parts of the body that have elasticity, e.g. the skin

emulsification   mixing liquids that do not normally mix, e.g. oil and water

energy density   the amount of energy calories (cal) or kilojoules (kJ) a food contains per gram

enriched dough   basic bread dough with the addition of sugar, butter and sometimes egg

enrobed   to cover a food stuff in a coating, e.g. breadcrumbs around fish

enzymes   biological catalysts found in all cells, usually made from protein; enzymes break down plant and animal tissues causing fruit to ripen, meat to tenderise and enzymic browning (also known as oxidation) to speed up

enzymic browning   browning of food due to enzymes in cut fruits and vegetables

essential amino acids   the eight amino acids that need to be provided in the diet for good health

Estimated Average Requirements (EARs)   tables used by nutritionists that provide guidelines to the energy needs of individuals at various stages of life

ethical   decisions or actions taken on the basis of strongly held moral beliefs or intellectual principles

evaporated   when a liquid is heated so that water is removed

F

Fair trade   an organisation dedicated to securing fair working, social and environmental conditions, sale prices and trade deals for farmers and manufacturers in developing countries

fat-soluble vitamins   these are vitamins A, D, E and K and they are stored in the body for longer periods than water-soluble vitamins

fatty acids   fat is made up of fatty acids and glycerol

field to fork   the name given to the food chain from the start of agricultural production to final consumption

filleting   a thin-bladed, flexible and very sharp knife used to fillet fish

fish farms   places where fish are commercially farmed

flexible   something that moves and bends easily

foam   the incorporation of a gas or air in a liquid, e.g. egg white foam

foetus   a baby still in the womb

food miles   the distances food travels from its point of origin to your table

food poisoning   illness caused by harmful bacteria (pathogens) multiplying in or on food; symptoms of food poisoning include stomach pains, diarrhoea, vomiting, nausea (feeling sick), and fever

food waste   food that is wasted by not being eaten or by being discarded; food can be discarded for many reasons, e.g. during production due to contamination or in supermarkets due to the expiration of use-by dates

fortified   strengthening the nutritional content of a food by adding vitamins and minerals

free-range farming   farming where the animals reared can roam freely outdoors for a portion of the day rather than being confined in a small space indoors 24 hours a day

frozen food   food that has been frozen as quickly as possible after it has been harvested or made and is kept frozen until it is required to be cooked for consumption

G

gelatine   a water-soluble protein that comes from collagen and is used in food preparation; it is colourless and tasteless

gelatinisation   chemical term for thickening by starch and starchy foods

gliadin   one of the two main components of the gluten fraction of the wheat seed (the other component is glutenin)

gluten   a protein found in wheat flour

glutenin   one of the two main components of the gluten fraction of the wheat seed (the other component is gliadin)

glycerol   part of a fat molecule

goujons   strips of chicken or fish that are deep-fried

Green House Gas (GHG)   any of a number of gases that absorb solar gases that contribute to the greenhouse effect, which contributes to global warming and climate change; examples include carbon dioxide, fluorocarbons, and methane

Genetically Modified (GM)   foods that have had changes introduced into their DNA using genetic engineering; GM foods can be manipulated to emphasise certain traits or to extinguish negative characteristics

H

haemoglobin   a red protein (it gives blood its colour) that transports oxygen around the body via red blood cells

halal   meat that can be eaten by Muslims because it has been killed in accordance with Islamic law

hatcheries   buildings/pools where fish or poultry eggs are artificially controlled and then hatched

heavy dropping consistency   when a mixture drops heavily from a spoon, rather than flowing from the spoon in a liquid or sticking to it in a lump

High Biological Value (HBV)   food sources, such as animal proteins, that contain all the essential amino acids required by the body

high-risk foods   foods that have a high risk of harbouring harmful bacteria, e.g. raw meat, raw seafood, cooked rice

homogenised   milk that is forced through tiny holes in a machine; this breaks up the fat and disperses it, and it doesn't reform as a layer

hydrogenation   making solid fat from a liquid oil

hydroponics   the name given to the process of growing plants without soil but in sand, gravel or liquid with nutrients added to stimulate growth

hygiene   the practice of preventing contamination by following strict cleanliness procedures

I

ingredients   single food items within a recipe

intensive farming   commercial agriculture on an industrial scale designed to maximise yields and profit; this type of farming relies on heavy use of pesticides and chemical fertilisers

iron-deficiency anaemia   a common condition in teenage girls who have started menstruating (the blood loss incurred by menstruation causes iron deficiency)

J

jardinière   ingredients cut into baton-shaped lengths

julienne   ingredients cut into matchstick-sized strips

K

kosher food that conforms to Jewish dietary law

kwashiorkor a severe form of protein malnutrition

L

lactating the production of milk by women from the mammary glands to feed new-born babies (all mammals lactate)

lacto vegetarian a person who eats only dairy foods, no eggs, meat or fish

lactose intolerance a condition where someone is intolerant of lactose, which is a natural sugar found in milk; lactose intolerance causes stomach upset

landfill waste disposed of via landfill is dumped into a massive hole in the ground and eventually buried

Low Biological Value (LBV) protein from plant sources is of Low Biological Value (LBV) and lacks some essential amino acids; the exception is soy, which is a plant protein of HBV

M

macédoine ingredients cut into medium-sized dice

Maillard reaction the browning of meat, caused by a reaction with natural sugars and proteins which produces a dark colour; also known as non-enzymic browning

malnutrition a significant lack of proper nutrition

manufacturer a company producing large quantities of food for sale to the public

marinade a mixture created to tenderise and flavour meat, fish and alternatives

menstruation the monthly process the human female body goes through to discharge the lining of the uterus; takes place from puberty to menopause

microorganisms another name for bacteria

microwave using a type of radiation called microwaves (produced by a magnetron), which travel in straight lines and penetrate food to cook or reheat it

milling the process whereby wheat is made into a flour; wheat grains are blended with other varieties and washed to remove grit and dirt then huge rotating rollers crush the grains at varying speeds – the crushed grain is sieved and this produces flour

mollusc oysters, mussels, scallops, winkles and cockles are all molluscs

monosaccharides the simplest form of carbohydrate structure

moulds a type of fungus that can settle on food and grow into a visible plant; a sign of food that is not fresh

multicultural foods from a variety of countries, regions and cultures

muscle fibre cells that give structure to muscles; different structures of muscle fibre indicate different types of muscle

myoglobin a protein found in most mammals that is oxygen-binding and protein-binding

N

non-enzymic browning browning due to caramelisation or dextrinisation, not caused by enzymes

Non-Starch Polysaccharide (NSP) the correct scientific name for fibre

nutrition labelling labels that show which nutrients a food product contains

O

olfactory relating to the sense of smell

organic food that is grown or produced without using chemical fertilisers or pesticides

origin where something first comes from

osteomalacia the name of the medical condition where bones become soft due to a lack of calcium or vitamin D

osteoporosis the name of a medical condition where bones become weak, brittle and break easily

ovo-lacto vegetarian vegetarians who eat eggs and dairy products (but only cheese that has been made with vegetable rennet)

oxidation changes in food such as colour change or flavour change due to exposure to oxygen

P

packaging the items used to wrap around foodstuffs; designed to protect and preserve

palatability to make food appealing through its appearance, colour, flavour, texture and smell

palate a person's ability to be able to distinguish between, and appreciate, different flavours

paring a small knife used to prepare fruit and vegetables

pasteurised a process of part sterilisation conducted via heat treatment or irradiation; pasteurisation makes food safer to eat and lengthens its shelf life

pathogens bacteria/microorganisms that cause disease

peak bone mass when bones reach their maximum strength

pH level the level of acidity or alkalinity of a food

photosynthesis the process that plants use to convert energy from sunlight into chemical energy that the plant can use to feed itself

Physical Activity Level (PAL) the energy needed by the body for movement of all types

physical raising methods using air, steam or water vapour to lighten and raise mixtures

plasticity how fat properties change over a range of temperatures

polysaccharides polysaccharides are made up of many monosaccharide units joined together

precise accurate

pre-packed food that has been packed before the customer buys it

preservation the process of altering a foodstuff so that it can be kept for as long as possible, e.g. canning, pickling

primary processing the conversion of foods in their raw state into other food products by combining the raw ingredient with other foods

probiotic probiotic cultures are carefully selected strains; there is good evidence that they help improve digestion, safeguard the immune system, and keep the body's intestinal flora in balance

proportions the parts of a food stuff comparative to the whole amount

protein complementation when the proteins of a LBV can be eaten together to provide all the essential amino acids, e.g. beans on toast

proving the last stage of rising bread goes through prior to baking

puberty the stage of life when adolescents mature and become capable of sexual reproduction

R

radiation heat transfer method, a type of electromagnetic radiation that involves waves, e.g. grill

rating assessing something in terms of quality, quantity or a combination of both

ratio proportion of ingredients in a basic recipe

recycling re-using/converting waste materials, including food

Red Tractor a logo that tells the consumer that the food has been produced, processed and packed to Red Tractor standards; it assures standards of food hygiene and safety; equipment used in production; animal health and welfare; environmental issues and responsible use of pesticides

Reference Intake (RI) the approximate amount of a nutrient provided by a portion of food

regional belonging to one particular geographical region

reheating to heat something again; reheated food should reach a core temperature of 75 °C

rest when a dough is left, usually in a fridge or similar cold location, for a period of time before it is baked

retailer an individual or organisation that sells goods

riboflavin another name for vitamin B2

rickets a childhood disease caused by a lack of vitamin D; it causes softening of the bones, which results in bow legs

rolling boil when something is boiling all over the surface (both middle and sides) with great energy

rubbing-in incorporating fat into flour when making pastry

S

salting the name given to the process of adding salt to a foodstuff to remove its moisture; food-poisoning bacteria cannot survive without moisture

saturated fats come mainly from animal food products, e.g. lard, and they are solid at room temperature; saturated fats raise your cholesterol level – too much bad cholesterol can lead to health problems

secondary processing the processing of raw food ingredients into other food products

semi-skimmed pasteurised milk that has had some of the cream removed

senses perception of a food using hearing, sight, touch, smell and taste

sensory analysis the application of sight, smell, taste, touch and hearing to evaluate foods

sensory characteristic using the senses to evaluate food products, e.g. aroma, texture

serrated a type of knife blade that is jagged; often used to carve joints of meat

shortcrust a type of pastry used for pies and tarts

shortening mouthfeel, such as short or crumbly, produced by short gluten strands

skimmed pasteurised milk that has had all or most of the cream removed

smoking the name given to the process of smoking a foodstuff to a temperature of 76 °C or above; this removes the moisture, extends shelf life, and imparts a distinctive flavour

spina bifida a defect of the lower spine which can result in paralysis in the legs and feet and is sometimes accompanied by learning difficulties

starter culture a mixture of flour and water that ferments with bacteria; a starter culture aids fermentation in bread making

sterilised subjecting a food to a high temperature to kill any bacteria that may be present; typically heating to between 110 °C and 135 °C takes place for 15–20 minutes

sustainable food food that will continue to be available for many years to come

T

taste sensation of flavour in the mouth on coming into contact with food

temperature a measure of intensity of heat or cold

texture properties of a food sensed by mouthfeel

thiamin another name for vitamin B1

thyroid this is a gland at the front your neck, just below the Adam's apple; it produces two hormones which control the body's metabolic rate

traceability knowing the history of a foodstuff from the place of its birth/planting all the way through its manufacturing journey to the consumer

trans fats trans fats can be formed when oil goes through the process of hydrogenation to form a solid; this process occurs as the molecules flip and rotate

transportation moving items or people from one place to another using various forms of transport, e.g. plane, lorry, boat

U

Ultra-Heat Treated (UHT) the process of heating food above a temperature of 135 °C; this sterilises the food and lengthens its shelf life

unsaturated fats come from plants, e.g. olive oil, and some animals; they are liquid at room temperature

use-by date a safety date found on foods and their packaging – the food must be eaten by the date on the packaging; found on highly perishable packaged food, e.g. meat

V

vegan a person who does not eat any animal or animal products

vegetarian a person who chooses not to eat foods which involve killing animals or fish

viscosity resistance to flow, thickness of a sauce or mixture

volume the amount of liquid in a container, e.g. milk in a measuring jug

Y

yeast a biological raising agent that ferments to produce carbon dioxide

Index

Collins

AQA GCSE 9-1
Food Preparation and Nutrition

Workbook

Fiona Balding, Barbara Monks,
Barbara Rathmill and
Suzanne Gray with Louise T. Davies

Preparing for the GCSE Exam

Revision That Really Works

Experts have found that there are two techniques that help you to retain and recall information and consistently produce better results in exams compared to other revision techniques.

It really isn't rocket science either – you simply need to:

- **test yourself** on each topic as many times as possible
- **leave a gap** between the test sessions.

Three Essential Revision Tips

1. **Use Your Time Wisely**

   - Allow yourself plenty of time.
   - Try to start revising at least six months before your exams – it's more effective and less stressful.
   - Don't waste time re-reading the same information over and over again – it's not effective!

2. **Make a Plan**

   - Identify all the topics you need to revise (this Complete Revision & Practice book will help you).
   - Plan at least five sessions for each topic.
   - One hour should be ample time to test yourself on the key ideas for a topic.
   - Spread out the practice sessions for each topic – the optimum time to leave between each session is about one month but, if this isn't possible, just make the gaps as big as realistically possible.

3. **Test Yourself**

   - Methods for testing yourself include: quizzes, practice questions, flashcards, past papers, explaining a topic to someone else, etc.
   - This Complete Revision & Practice book provides seven practice opportunities per topic.
   - Don't worry if you get an answer wrong – provided you check what the correct answer is, you are more likely to get the same or similar questions right in future!

Visit **collins.co.uk/collinsGCSErevision** to download your free flashcards, for more information about the benefits of these techniques, and for further guidance on how to plan ahead and make them work for you.

Command Words Used in Exam Questions

This table shows the meanings of some of the most commonly used command words in GCSE exam questions.

Command word	Meaning
State…/Give…	Write the facts clearly and briefly, giving your answer from recall.
Name…	Write the correct name or term.
Which…	Choose the correct option from the information given.
Describe…	Give clear characteristics in sufficient detail.
Explain…	Write a detailed answer using appropriate terminology to give reasons.
Discuss…	Write about the different points of view or the strengths and weaknesses. Give the key points about the topic.
Compare…	Write about the similarities and differences in the information you are given.
Suggest…	Present ideas that are reasonable and sensible.
Complete…	Add to a task to finalise or finish it off.
Interpret…	Understand and make sense of the information provided to answer the question.
Review…	Interpret and evaluate the information given.

Contents

1 Which type of knife is shown in the picture? Tick the correct answer.

   a) Paring knife ☐   **b)** Filleting knife ☐

   c) Cook's knife ☐   **d)** Palette knife ☐   **[1]**

2 When preparing meat, what colour cutting board should be used? Tick the correct answer.

   a) Blue ☐   **b)** Green ☐

   c) Brown ☐   **d)** Red ☐   **[1]**

3 Explain three important safety rules to observe when using knives for preparing different foods.

Safety Rule 1: ....

Reason: ....

Safety Rule 2: ....

Reason: ....

Safety Rule 3: ....

Reason: .... **[6]**

4 Good knife skills are the foundation of many cooking techniques to produce high quality dishes. Name and describe the two main methods of cutting that are the basis of a cook's knife-handling skills.

	Knife Hold: ....
	Explanation: ....
	Knife Hold: ....
	Explanation: ....

[4]

Total Marks .... **/ 12**

1 Which of the following fish would you expect to find preserved in a can? Tick the correct answer.

a) Cod ☐   b) Plaice ☐

c) Salmon ☐   d) Halibut ☐   [1]

2 Which choice would **not** be suitable when enrobing a fish fillet before cooking? Tick the correct answer.

a) Breadcrumbs ☐   b) Polenta ☐

c) Batter ☐   d) Roux sauce ☐   [1]

3 Complete the following statements using the words below.

| collagen | 60 °C | coagulate | muscle | gelatine | connective tissue |

Fish cooks quickly because the _____ is short and the

_____ is thin.

The connective tissue is made up of _____ and will change into

_____ and _____ at _____.   [6]

4 Answer the questions about the fish shown.

a) What is the classification of the fish? _____ [1]

b) Give one example of this type of fish. _____ [1]

c) What type of knife should be used to prepare this fish? _____ [1]

d) What colour chopping board should be used to prepare this fish? _____ [1]

e) Explain how you would fillet this fish.

_____

_____

_____

_____

_____   [3]

Total Marks _____ / 15

1 Which of these nutrients is **not** found in meat? Tick the correct answer.

a) Fat ☐ **b)** Calcium ☐

c) Vitamin B6 ☐ **d)** Vitamin E ☐ [1]

2 Which meat is classed as game? Tick the correct answer.

a) Duck ☐ **b)** Beef ☐

c) Pheasant ☐ **d)** Chicken ☐ [1]

3 Some meats cuts are more tender than others. Name one cut of meat that is tough and discuss two different methods that could be used for cooking to ensure it is tender.

....

....

....

....

[3]

4 What colour board should be used to prepare raw meat? .... [1]

5 Name two methods of tenderising meat.

....

....

[2]

6 Complete the following sentences about what happens when meat is cooked. Use the words below.

| Maillard | gelatine | coagulate | browning | sugars |

The .... of meat is caused by a reaction with natural .... and

proteins to produce a dark colour. This occurrence is called the .... reaction or

non-enzymic browning.

As the meat cooks, the proteins .... and produce a firm texture. Collagen is

broken down into .... [5]

Total Marks .... / 13

1 Which glaze would be most suitable for plain bread rolls? Tick the correct answer.

a) Egg wash ☐   b) Sugar and water ☐

c) Arrowroot glaze ☐   d) Salt water ☐   [1]

2 The following sentences describe the technique of folding in flour.

Choose the correct words from the boxes to complete the sentences.

| combine | figure-of-eight | texture | mix | cake | retains |

Folding and stirring are methods used to .... and ....

ingredients. Folding is different to stirring because it is a careful .... movement

used for adding flour when .... making. Folding .... air in a

cake mixture, which helps the cooked cake to have a light, airy ....   [6]

3 Biscuits and some types of bread need skilled handling and special techniques to achieve their distinctive shapes.

a) Which piece of equipment would ensure consistent even thickness for biscuits?

....   [1]

b) The picture shows Palmier biscuits. Name the two techniques used to achieve their shape.

....   [2]

c) The picture shows Viennese whirl biscuits. What method is used to achieve their shape?

....   [2]

d) The picture shows some wholegrain bread rolls. What methods would be used to achieve their shape?

....   [3]

Total Marks .... / 15

1 a) How can pasta dough be rolled consistently and evenly?

.... [1]

b) After pasta is rolled, cut and left to air dry, what changes occur?

.... [2]

2 Which one of the following would be the best choice of flour for making pasta dough? Tick the correct answer.

a) Self-raising wheat flour ☐   **b)** '00' Durum wheat flour ☐

c) Cornflour ☐   **d)** Gram flour ☐

e) Rice flour ☐ [1]

3 Name two ingredients that could be successfully used to add colour to pasta dough.

Ingredient: ....   Colour achieved: ....

Ingredient: ....   Colour achieved: .... [4]

4 Flour-based mixtures are popular when learning to cook. Circle which of the following are flour-based recipes.

[3]

Omelette   **Pastry**   **Porridge**   **Bread**   **Pasta**   **Risotto**   **Ratatouille**

5 Choux pastry contains fat. Explain how the fat is prepared to be added to the flour.

....

.... [2]

6 Shortcrust pastry is made with a ratio of half fat to flour. True or False?

.... [1]

Total Marks .... / 14

1. Proteins are formed from units called a... a... .   [2]

2. a) Give three good sources of plant protein.

   ....

   ....   [3]

   b) Circle two of the following dishes that would be a good protein source for a lacto vegetarian.

   Fish Pie   **Cauliflower Cheese**   **Chicken and Chickpea Curry**

   Mushroom and Lentil Bake   [2]

3. What is Protein Complementation? Give an example.

   ....

   ....

   ....   [2]

4. Fats are made of f........................ a........................ and g........................ .   [2]

5. Saturated fats can increase what level in the blood? Tick the correct answer.

   a) Iron   ☐

   b) Blood sugar   ☐

   c) Cholesterol   ☐

   d) Amino acids   ☐   [1]

6. Give three examples of foods which are high in unsaturated fat.

   ....

   ....

   ....   [3]

   Total Marks .... / 15

Carbohydrate

1. The main function of carbohydrate in the body is to provide _____. [1]

2. Carbohydrates are produced mainly by plants during what process? Circle the correct answer.

   Osmosis   **Dextrinisation**   **Photosynthesis**   **Caramelisation**   [1]

3. A lack of fibre in the diet can cause the medical condition constipation. Explain what this condition is.

   ....

   ....

   .... [2]

4. How much dietary fibre is recommended for an adult every day? Tick the correct answer.

   a) A least 6 g ☐   b) At least 10 g ☐

   c) At least 18 g ☐   d) At least 30 g ☐   [1]

5. Carbohydrates can be classified according to their structure.

   Those structures are:

   M..

   D..

   P.. [3]

6. Explain why starches provide slow-release energy in the body.

   ....

   ....

   .... [2]

7. Discuss the health implications of consuming too much carbohydrate.

   ....

   ....

   ....

   ....

   .... [3]

   Total Marks _____ / 13

Vitamins

1 Name three dietary sources of Vitamin C.

....

....

....   [3]

2 Which vitamin can be made in the body by the action of sunlight on the skin?

Tick the correct answer.

a) Vitamin B1   ☐

b) Vitamin D   ☐

c) Vitamin A   ☐

d) Vitamin E   ☐   [1]

3 Spina bifida has been linked to a lack of which vitamin, both pre and during pregnancy?

....   [1]

4 Water soluble Vitamins B and C can be lost easily during food preparation and cooking. Suggest three ways to maximise vitamin retention.

....

....

....

....   [3]

5 The table below lists five vitamins. Give one function of each.

Vitamin	Function
Vitamin A	
Vitamin K	
Vitamin C	
Vitamin D	
Vitamin B1	

[5]

Total Marks .... / 13

Minerals and Water

1 Vitamin C assists with the absorption of which mineral in the body? Underline the correct answer.

Calcium   Iodine   Sodium   Iron   [1]

2 Fill in the missing words to complete the sentence.

Iron supports the production of h........................... in red blood cells, which transport

o........................... around the body.   [2]

3 **a)** Lack of water, particularly during hot weather, can cause what condition?

.... [1]

b) Give three functions of water in the body.

....

....

.... [3]

4 Two deficiency diseases associated with a lack of calcium in the diet are:

R........................... in children.

O........................... in older people.   [2]

5 Give three good sources of iron in the diet.

....

....

.... [3]

> **Total Marks** .... / 12

1 Referring to the Eatwell Guide, which two sections are the largest?

....

.... [2]

2 Fill in the missing words to complete the sentence.

For breast-fed babies, the first milk that a mother produces is called c................................

and it is full of a.. . [2]

3 Why is iron-deficiency anaemia common in teenage girls?

....

....

.... [2]

4 Older people require a good supply of calcium in the diet to help prevent which condition?
Underline the correct answer.

Anaemia　　　　　**Scurvy**　　　　　**Dementia**　　　　　**Osteoporosis**　　　[1]

5 Name two plant sources of protein that could be found in the pink section of the Eatwell Guide.

....

.... [2]

6 It is important that pregnant women have a healthy diet. Name three nutrients that they need to increase their consumption of, and explain why they are important for the developing baby.

....

....

....

....

....

.... [6]

> **Total Marks** .... / 15

1 Fill in the missing word.

_____ is an abnormal accumulation of body fat. [1]

2 What is used as a measurement in adults to see if they are a healthy weight for their height?

_____ [1]

3 Explain why elderly people require a good supply of calcium and Vitamin D.

_____

_____

_____ [2]

4 The risk of bowel cancer can be reduced by increasing what in the diet? Circle the correct answer.

Sugar   Fibre/NSP   Protein   Vitamin C   [1]

5 Explain the damage that can be caused to children's teeth as a result of a high sugar diet.

_____

_____

_____

_____ [2]

6 Give three symptoms of iron-deficient anaemia.

_____

_____

_____ [3]

7 Fill in the missing words to complete the sentences.

In Type 2 d_____, too little or no i_____ is produced in the

p_____ resulting in high levels of s_____ in the b_____. [5]

Total Marks _____ / 15

Cooking of Food, Heat Transfer and Selecting Appropriate Cooking Methods

1 A chef has to decide between oven-roasting a range of vegetables or boiling the same vegetables. What characteristics would be different after cooking in each way?

Oven-roasted Vegetables	Boiled Vegetables

[4]

2 What is the correct heat transfer method for frying onions? Tick the correct answer.

a) Conduction ☐   b) Convection ☐

c) Radiation ☐   d) Induction ☐   [1]

3 Boiled potatoes can be mashed and layered over a meat mixture, such as in cottage pie. Which cooking method and heat transfer method would change the plain mashed potato topping to become golden brown and crisp?

[2]

4 A menu in a restaurant offers poached salmon and marinated chicken thighs.

a) Describe the main effect of poaching the salmon.   [2]

b) State the main reasons for marinating the chicken thighs.

[2]

5 Complete the following sentences using the words given below.

sticking	convection	heat	conduction	thickening

When making a sauce, heat is transferred from the hob through the base of the pan by

_____ and through the sauce by _____. Stirring prevents

_____ on the base of the pan and distributes _____ to aid

_____.

[5]

Total Marks _____ / 16

1 When making a pear flan with fresh fruit, the topping starts to turn brown.

a) Explain why the pears turn brown.

_____

_____ [2]

b) Suggest what could stop the browning of the pears.

_____ [1]

2 Bread and butter pudding is an affordable and nutritious pudding. Buttered bread is soaked in an egg custard mixture before cooking.

a) State two changes that would be seen when the pudding is cooked.

_____

_____ [2]

b) Explain how and why the egg and milk custard is changed by the cooking.

_____

_____

_____

_____ [4]

3 a) Name the enzyme present in fresh pineapple.

_____ [1]

b) What purpose would fresh pineapple have if used in a marinade for prawns before cooking?

_____ [1]

4 Which of the following would reduce oxidation occurring when cooking vegetables? Tick the correct answers.

a) Using bicarbonate of soda in the cooking water ☐

b) Using a lid on the pan when boiling vegetables ☐

c) Using quicker short methods of cooking such as microwave or stir-fry ☐ [2]

5 Which protein helps a dough to be stretchy and elastic? Circle the correct answer. [1]

Glucose   **Glycerine**   **Gluten**   **Glycerol**

Total Marks _____ / 14

1 A recipe asks for onions to be sliced and fried gently until golden. What are the reasons for this?

....

....

.... **[3]**

2 a) When making soup from vegetables and a stock, name two different starches that could be used as thickeners.

.... **[2]**

b) Explain how starch can thicken a liquid.

....

....

.... **[3]**

3 When making toast, describe how sensory factors are changed because of grilling.

....

.... **[2]**

4 a) What are the reasons for a roux sauce being stirred throughout preparation?

....

....

.... **[4]**

b) Which two methods of sauce making bring about gelatinisation of starch? Tick the two correct answers.

i) Emulsification ☐

ii) Blending ☐

iii) Reduction ☐

iv) Roux ☐ **[2]**

Total Marks _____ / 16

1 Here is a shortbread recipe. Explain the functions of the baking fat in this recipe.

150 g flour
100 g baking fat (yellow fat)
50 g caster sugar

....

....

....

....

[4]

2 When using baking fat, such as butter, temperature plays an important role.

a) Insert the following food preparation methods in the correct place in the table.

Creaming   Rubbing-in   Melting method   [3]

Temperature of Fat	Food Preparation Method	Example of Dish
Chilled temperature		
Room temperature		
Warm pan temperature		

b) Complete the chart by giving an example of a dish made using each preparation method.

[3]

3 a) When making cakes, why is aeration so important? Give two reasons.

....

....

[2]

b) Name two cake preparation methods that aerate mixtures effectively.

....

....

[2]

4 What sort of foam is achieved when a creaming method is successfully prepared?

....

[1]

Total Marks .... / 15

1 **a)** A student is researching mechanical (physical) methods of raising agents by preparing a range of dishes.

Complete the list in the table below by naming a recipe and linking it to a method of trapping air. The first one has been done for you:

Recipe/Product Name	Mechanical (Physical) Method to Trap Air
Pastry	*Rubbing-in technique*

[4]

b) Name and give an example of one other classification of raising agents that is **not** biological.

.... [2]

2 Choose the most likely raising method from the list below, for successful use in the preparation of the products in the table.

Steam production   Beating   S.R. flour   Baking powder

Product	Raising Agent
Victoria sandwich	
Muffins	
English pancakes	
Choux buns	

[4]

3 Which raising agent is particularly likely to give a soapy taste to products?

.... [1]

4 What type of foam does egg white produce when whisked?

.... [1]

5 What is baking powder?

....

.... [4]

Total Marks .... / 16

1 Name two microorganisms that can cause food spoilage.

.... [2]

2 Give three factors that affect the rate of microbial growth.

....

.... [3]

3 Identify three signs that could show if food has spoiled.

....

....

.... [3]

4 Suggest three ways to store dry food, such as flour, in order to stop it from spoiling.

....

....

.... [3]

5 Suggest two ways in which oxidation (enzymic browning), as shown in the picture, can be prevented.

....

.... [2]

Total Marks .... / 13

Microorganisms in Food Production

1 Complete the following sentences using the words below.

| probiotic | harmful | digestion | single | rapidly |

| cheese | food poisoning |

Bacteria are _____-celled organisms, which are able to reproduce

_____. Some are _____ and cause _____

or even death. Some are harmless and used in _____-making.

_____ bacteria help _____.   [7]

2 Discuss the positive uses of the following microorganisms on food production. Use examples in your answer.

a) Moulds

_____

_____

_____

_____

_____

_____   [4]

b) Bacteria

_____

_____

_____

_____

_____   [4]

3 Starter cultures are used to make dried, fermented meat products. Give three examples of these products.

_____

_____   [3]

Total Marks _____ / 18

Bacterial Contamination

1 Complete this table relating to food poisoning, giving one food source and one symptom for each type of food-poisoning bacteria.

Name of Bacteria	One Food Source	One Symptom
E-Coli		
Campylobacter		
Bacillus Cereus		
Staphylococcus Aureus		

[8]

2 Explain why food-borne disease is different from food-poisoning bacteria.

....

....

....

....

....

[2]

3 Bacteria will grow if food is stored incorrectly.

Give three conditions bacteria need in order to grow.

....

....

....

....

[3]

Total Marks .... / 13

Buying and Storing Food

Video Solution   Question 2

1 Explain the importance of storing high-risk foods correctly.

....

....

....

....

....

....

....

....

.... [4]

2 Give two food safety rules that must be followed when storing fresh fish.

Explain why each rule is needed.

Food Safety Rule	Explanation

[4]

3 If warm food is put into a refrigerator, the temperature inside the fridge will rise. What temperature range is classed as the danger zone in the fridge?
Tick the correct answer.

a) 1–4°C ☐

b) 10–72°C ☐

c) 8–13°C ☐

d) 5–63°C ☐

[1]

Total Marks .... / 9

1 State four personal hygiene rules that must be followed by people when preparing and cooking food.

....

....

....

....

....

....

....

.... [4]

2 Care must be taken when preparing and cooking high-risk foods. Give three examples of high-risk foods.

....

....

.... [3]

3 It is important to prepare and cook food at the correct temperature.

Name one piece of equipment used to check the temperature of a joint of meat whilst it is being cooked.

.... [1]

4 Keeping food hot for serving is important for food safety. What is the correct temperature a chicken curry must be kept at in a school canteen?
Tick the correct answer.

a) 30°C ☐

b) 45°C ☐

c) 63°C ☐

d) 90°C ☐ [1]

Total Marks .... / 9

Food Choices

Food Choices

1 What is the only type of meat allowed in Judaism?

_____ [1]

2 An allergy to nuts could cause what reaction? Underline the correct answer.

Fainting   Anaphylaxis   Itchy scalp   Nose bleed   [1]

3 Explain what Coeliac disease is.

_____

_____

_____ [3]

4 What is the name of the condition that occurs when someone cannot digest the sugars found in milk and milk products?

_____ [1]

5 What do you understand by this symbol?

_____

_____ [1]

6 Complete the table.

Religion	Dietary Restriction
	No pork, only Halal meat
	No beef or beef products
	No particular dietary restrictions

[3]

7 Explain the differences between Type 1 and Type 2 diabetes.

_____

_____

_____ [3]

Total Marks _____ / 13

British and International Cuisines

1 Tick one answer. 'Cuisine' relates to:

a) The way in which food is cooked in a kitchen. ☐

b) The range of dishes and foods of a particular country or region. ☐

c) The information listed on a food label. ☐

[1]

2 Which British cheese originates from Somerset? Circle the correct answer.

Stilton　　　**Cheddar**　　　**Double Gloucester**　　　**Red Leicester**

[1]

3 Traditional dishes are important in any society as they originate from the ingredients grown in that country or region, the local climate and traditions.

Write the dishes below next to the correct country in the table and describe the key ingredients and flavours of the dish.

Tortilla　　　**Cornish pasty**　　　**Minestrone**　　　**Bouillabaisse**

Shepherd's pie　　　**Lasagne**　　　**Paella**　　　**Tarte tatin**

Country	Dish	Key Ingredients and Flavours	
England			[4]
France			[4]
Spain			[4]
Italy			[4]

Total Marks _____ / 18

1 Complete the following sentence using the words below.

| together | five | evaluate | like | eat | analysis |

Sensory _____ involves using our _____ senses to

_____ how much we _____ a dish. We use these senses

_____ when we _____ our food.   [6]

2 When tasting food, what are the five basic senses?

_____

_____   [5]

3 Describe how to set up a tasting area to trial your practical work in the food room.

_____

_____

_____

_____

_____

_____

_____   [6]

4 What do you understand by a 'triangle test'?

_____

_____

_____   [4]

5 What does a preference test aim to find out? Tick the correct answer.

a) The sensory characteristics of a food product.   ☐

b) Whether consumers like or dislike a food product.   ☐

c) If any differences occur between two products.   ☐

d) The dominance of a sensory feature, such as crunchiness.   ☐   [1]

Total Marks _____ / 22

1 Which food label indicates that the food should no longer be offered for sale in a shop? Tick the correct answer.

a) Use by ☐

b) Best before ☐

c) Display until ☐

d) Sell by ☐

[1]

2 What does GDA stand for?

.... [1]

3 How are ingredients listed on a food label?

.... [1]

4 Other than the ingredients, what other information must legally be present on a food label? Give six examples.

....

....

....

....

....

.... [6]

5 Explain how the 14 identified allergens must be displayed on a food label.

....

....

.... [2]

Total Marks _____ / 11

Factors Affecting Food Choice

Video Solution

Question 5

1 Fill in the missing words to complete the sentence.

Our enjoyment of food is affected by what the food l............................, s............................

and t............................ like. **[3]**

2 Give three examples of foods that are specifically eaten at religious festivals.

....

....

.... **[3]**

3 Give three advantages of eating locally produced foods in season.

....

....

....

.... **[3]**

4 Circle the correct answer.

Fresh strawberries brought in a supermarket in December are most likely to have been…

exported **genetically modified** **imported** **irradiated** **[1]**

5 Supermarkets and food retailers can influence the food we buy. Discuss the marketing strategies they could use to influence the consumers' food choice.

....

....

....

....

.... **[3]**

Total Marks .... / 13

Food and the Environment

1 Name two dishes that use up leftover food.

_____ [2]

2 What gas does waste food give off as it decomposes in landfill? Tick the correct answer.

a) Hydrogen ☐

b) Carbon monoxide ☐

c) Methane ☐

d) Carbon dioxide ☐ [1]

3 What is sustainable food? Tick the correct answer.

a) Food that lasts longer in the fridge. ☐

b) Food that will continue to be available for many years to come. ☐

c) Food that is grown nearby. ☐

d) Food that does not need to be stored in the fridge or freezer. ☐ [1]

4 Home composting is efficient, easy and clean.

What two things are needed in order to return goodness to the soil?

_____ [2]

5 When you throw away food, you waste not only the food but also the resources – such as energy, fuel and water – that went into growing, harvesting, transporting and storing the food. Discarded food then goes on to produce gas in landfill sites.

Discuss what every person can do to prevent this food waste.

_____

_____

_____

_____

_____

_____

_____ [6]

Total Marks _____ / 12

Food Provenance and Production Methods

1. What are organic foods? Tick the correct answer.

   a) Foods that have been genetically modified.   ☐

   b) Foods that are grown for people who are vegan.   ☐

   c) Foods that are grown reliant on natural composts and manure as fertilisers.   ☐

   d) Foods that are proven to be better for us to eat.   ☐   [1]

2. Explain what hydroponic farming is.

   ....

   ....

   ....

   ....   [4]

3. What concerns are there about GM (Genetically Modified) food production?
   Tick the correct answers.

   a) It is more expensive.   ☐

   b) There is a possibility of new strains of microorganisms developing.   ☐

   c) It is altering and playing with nature.   ☐

   d) It is less resistant to plant disease.   ☐

   e) It is not monitored.   ☐   [2]

4. In the food chain, name five people who have responsibility for food safety.

   ....

   ....   [5]

5. After the Second World War, intensive farming became popular as farmers were offered subsidies to farm large scale, low cost products.
   Give three effects that this policy has had on the food chain.

   ....

   ....

   ....

   ....   [3]

Total Marks .... / 15

1 What does GHG stand for? Tick the correct answer.

    a) Good Health Guide ☐

    b) Greenhouse Gas ☐

    c) Growing High Greens ☐

    d) Government Health Group ☐

      [1]

2 Livestock, especially cows, produce methane gas which is 20 times more harmful than CO_2. True or false?

      [1]

3 **a)** What does Fairtrade mean?

      [2]

    b) Give two examples of foods that could display this logo.

      [1]

4 What are the advantages of buying a pack of pork chops that displays the Red Tractor logo and the British Flag?

      [8]

Total Marks _____ / 13

Video Solution   Question 3

1 What is condensed milk?

....

.... [1]

2 After the fat is removed from milk, it is used to make cream.

Name three different types of cream.

....

.... [3]

3 a) Name three regional varieties of cheese from the UK.

.... [3]

b) Name three French cheeses.

.... [3]

4 What is the name of the wheat used to make pasta flour?

.... [1]

5 a) What is the name of the outer layer of a grain of wheat?

.... [1]

b) When this is removed, what kind of flour is produced?

.... [1]

6 In the UK we drink mainly milk from cows, but it can also come from a variety of plant sources. Explain why some groups of people may choose to drink plant-based milk and give some examples of sources of this milk.

....

....

....

....

.... [4]

Total Marks .... / 17

Video Solution | Question 3

1 Name four different methods of drying foods to preserve them.

....

.... [4]

2 **a)** When milk is UHT treated, what does this mean?

....

.... [2]

b) What do the letters UHT stand for?

.... [1]

c) When milk is UHT treated, what changes occur?

....

....

.... [3]

3 Fruits and vegetables that are transported to this country from abroad are often irradiated.

a) What does irradiated mean?

....

.... [2]

b) What changes to vitamin content may this cause?

....

.... [4]

c) Does this affect the sensory attributes of the foods?

....

.... [2]

Total Marks .... / 18

Collins

GCSE
Food Preparation And Nutrition

Practice Paper 1

Materials

Time allowed: 1 hour 45 minutes

> **For this paper you must have:**
> - a black pen
> - a pencil.

Instructions

- Use black ink or black ball-point pen.
- Answer **all** questions.
- You must answer the questions in the spaces provided. Do not write outside the box around each page or on blank pages.
- Do all rough work in this answer book. Cross through any work you do not want to be marked.

Information

- The marks for questions are shown in brackets.
- The maximum mark for this paper is 100.
- You are reminded of the need for good English and clear presentation in your answers.

Name: ....

Practice Exam Paper 1

Section A consists of multiple choice questions.

There are 20 marks available.
Answer all questions.

For each question you should shade in **one** box.

An example is shown below.

Which food is high in fat?

A Bread ○

B Cheese ●

C Broccoli ○

D Apple ○

Question 1 is about diet, nutrition and health.

0 1 · 1 Citrus fruits are an excellent source of:

A Calcium ◯

B Vitamin C ◯

C Vitamin B ◯

D Calories ◯ [1 mark]

0 1 · 2 Which vitamin is needed to help prevent a birth defect called Spina bifida?

A Vitamin D ◯

B Vitamin A ◯

C Folic acid ◯

D Vitamin E ◯ [1 mark]

0 1 · 3 Retinol is an alternative name for which vitamin?

A Vitamin A ◯

B Vitamin C ◯

C Vitamin B2 ◯

D Vitamin K ◯ [1 mark]

0 1 · 4 What is the name of the medical condition, common in elderly people, when bones become weak, brittle and break easily?

A Anaemia ◯

B Angina ◯

C Osteoporosis ◯

D Diabetes ◯ [1 mark]

Practice Exam Paper 1

Question 2 is about food safety.

0 2 · 1 What is the temperature range regarded as the danger zone?

    A −10°C–20°C ⬜

    B 0°C–70°C ⬜

    C 5°C–63°C ⬜

    D 5°C–45°C ⬜ **[1 mark]**

0 2 · 2 Which one of the following is the primary cause of food-borne illness in the UK and most often associated with undercooked chicken?

    A Bacillus cereus ⬜

    B Listeria ⬜

    C E-Coli ⬜

    D Campylobacter jejuni ⬜ **[1 mark]**

0 2 · 3 Which one of the following does bacteria need in order to multiply?

    A Acid ⬜

    B Cold ⬜

    C Moisture ⬜

    D Salt ⬜ **[1 mark]**

0 2 · 4 Which one of the following statements is true? Food is cooked to:

    A make it easier to eat after cooking. ⬜

    B change the appearance of the food. ⬜

    C make it safe to eat. ⬜

    D combine proteins, fats and carbohydrates. ⬜ **[1 mark]**

Question 3 is about food science.

0 3 . 1 What causes the ripening and browning of bananas?

    A Enzyme activity ◯

    B Pathogens ◯

    C Sensory factors ◯

    D Contamination ◯   **[1 mark]**

0 3 . 2 What happens to fish flesh proteins during cooking?

    A Proteins are gelatinised. ◯

    B Proteins are denatured by heat. ◯

    C Proteins are homogenised. ◯

    D Proteins are rehydrated. ◯   **[1 mark]**

0 3 . 3 Béchamel sauce needs a flavoured milk. How is flavour imparted into the milk?

    A It is agitated. ◯

    B It is poached. ◯

    C It is stewed. ◯

    D It is infused. ◯   **[1 mark]**

0 3 . 4 A sauce recipe lists flour, milk and fat. What is the role of the flour?

    A Thickener ◯

    B Flavouring ◯

    C Colour ◯

    D Enriching ◯   **[1 mark]**

Practice Exam Paper 1

Question 4 is about food provenance.

| 0 4 . 1 | What are food miles?

    A The distance to the takeaway from your home. ◯

    B The distance that you travel to get to the local supermarket. ◯

    C The distance that food travels from its point of origin to your table. ◯

    D The distance that food travels from its point of origin to the supermarket. ◯ **[1 mark]**

| 0 4 . 2 | What is free-range farming?

    A A farm using large fields with no hedgerows or fencing. ◯

    B A farm where animals live in huge barns for their entire life. ◯

    C A farm where animals can access outdoor areas for part of their life. ◯

    D A farm where animals can access outdoor areas for their entire life. ◯ **[1 mark]**

| 0 4 . 3 | Cream is a by-product of milk. Which of the following types of cream is most suitable for piping?

    A Double ◯

    B Single ◯

    C Crème fraiche ◯

    D Sour cream ◯ **[1 mark]**

| 0 4 . 4 | Canning is a common method for high temperature storage of milk. Which milk is bought in cans?

    A Sterilised ◯

    B Condensed ◯

    C Pasteurised ◯

    D Ultra-Heat Treated (UHT) ◯ **[1 mark]**

Question 5 is about food choices.

0 5 · 1 Current Healthy Eating Guidelines recommend that we should eat how many portions of fruit and vegetables every day?

A 3–5 ◯

B 4–6 ◯

C 5–7 ◯

D 6–8 ◯ [1 mark]

0 5 · 2 Which section do potatoes belong to on the Eatwell Guide?

A Blue – dairy and alternatives. ◯

B Green – fruit and vegetables. ◯

C Purple – oils and spreads. ◯

D Yellow – starchy carbohydrates. ◯ [1 mark]

0 5 · 3 Which of the following foods is high in dietary fibre?

A Wholemeal bread ◯

B Chicken ◯

C Eggs ◯

D Tomato ketchup ◯ [1 mark]

0 5 · 4 Type 1 diabetes is a condition in which:

A the pancreas makes too much glycogen. ◯

B the stomach cannot digest sugar. ◯

C the pancreas makes too much insulin. ◯

D the pancreas makes no insulin. ◯ [1 mark]

Practice Exam Paper 1

Section B

Answer all questions in this section.
There are 80 marks available.

Question 6 is about diet, nutrition and health.

0 6 . 1 Give four reasons why it is important to follow the guidance of the Eatwell Guide.

....

....

....

....

[4 marks]

0 6 . 2 State three reasons why someone may not be able to follow the guidance of the Eatwell Guide.

....

....

....

[3 marks]

0 6 · 3 Explain the dietary advice you would give to women to ensure a healthy pregnancy and healthy newborn baby.

_____

_____

_____

_____

_____

_____

_____

_____

_____

_____

_____

[10 marks]

Practice Exam Paper 1

Question 7 is about carbohydrates and food preparation.

`0 7`·`1` Discuss the reasons for cooking and the changes brought about by boiling potatoes, rice and dried pasta.

....

....

....

....

[4 marks]

`0 7`·`2` Compare the two sauce recipes below and explain which would make the best sauce to pour and flow over a pudding.

| Sauce A | 250ml milk, 15g fat, 15g flour |
| Sauce B | 250ml milk, 30g fat, 30g flour |

....

....

....

[3 marks]

`0 7`·`3` On the chart provided, show how Sauce A would be different to Sauce B when tested for viscosity.

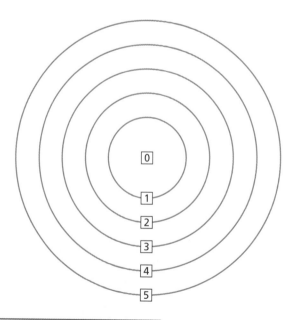

[2 marks]

0 7 · 4 Potatoes needed for making fishcakes are prepared according to the steps in the chart below. State the reasons for each of the stages. One has been completed for you.

Preparation and Cooking Stages	Reasons
Peel old potatoes.	*To remove dirt and skin to speed up cooking.*
Chop potatoes.	
Boil potatoes.	
Mash cooked potatoes.	

[3 marks]

0 7 · 5 Explain scientifically how the texture of mashed potato spread over the surface of fish pie could be changed by grilling.

....

....

[3 marks]

Question 8 is about food safety and food labelling.

0 8 . 1 Legally, food products must have the name of the product printed on the label. State six other items of information that must be given by law.

[6 marks]

0 8 . 2 Consumers use information from the labels of food products when choosing what to buy.

Here are some ingredients used in a ready-made quiche.

Ingredients:

100g plain flour, 60g chopped onion, 125ml egg, 75g grated cheese, 50g butter, 73ml water, 150ml milk, 10g chopped parsley

How would they appear on an ingredients list?

[6 marks]

0 8 . 3 Why is it important to include the manufacturer's name and address on the label?

[1 mark]

Question 9 is about sensory evaluation.

0 9 . 1 Give two reasons why sensory evaluation is carried out by food manufacturers.

[2 marks]

0 9 . 2 Explain why testers should have a glass of water when they are tasting food products.

[1 mark]

0 9 . 3 Describe how you would carry out a sensory analysis test to compare a cook-chill cottage pie and a homemade cottage pie.

[4 marks]

Practice Exam Paper 1

Question 10 is about cooking food, heat transfer and selecting appropriate cooking methods.

Here is a recipe list for a pasta bake.

Dried fusilli pasta
Homemade roux sauce
Grated cheddar cheese with breadcrumbs
Oven-roasted vegetables

1 0 . 1 Which cooking method would you select to cook the pasta and why?

[3 marks]

1 0 . 2 Give three reasons why it is important to stir a flour-based roux sauce when cooking it.

[3 marks]

1 0 . 3 Which heat transfer method would be most appropriate to ensure the top of the pasta bake is golden brown and crisp?

[2 marks]

1 0 · **4** Explain what is meant by oven-roasted vegetables and discuss the different characteristics they would have compared with boiled vegetables.

....

....

....

....

[4 marks]

Question 11 is about provenance and sustainability.

Food miles are the distance that our food travels from its point of origin to your table.

$1\ 1\ .\ 1$ Suggest two ways that we can reduce food miles.

[2 marks]

$1\ 1\ .\ 2$ Discuss why we are concerned about the distance our food has travelled before it is cooked and eaten.

[4 marks]

Question 12 is about provenance and sustainability.

12.1 All food must be traceable from field to fork.

Just before Easter 2022, a brand of chocolate eggs were discovered to possibly contain salmonella. Some batches had a recall notice issued.

What regulations are in place for manufacturers and the Food Standards Agency to ensure that recalls don't happen and that foods are safe?

[10 marks]

END OF QUESTIONS

Collins

GCSE
Food Preparation And Nutrition

Practice Paper 2

Materials

Time allowed: 1 hour 45 minutes

For this paper you must have:

- a black pen
- a pencil.

Instructions

- Use black ink or black ball-point pen.
- Answer **all** questions.
- You must answer the questions in the spaces provided. Do not write outside the box around each page or on blank pages.
- Do all rough work in this answer book. Cross through any work you do not want to be marked.

Information

- The marks for questions are shown in brackets.
- The maximum mark for this paper is 100.
- You are reminded of the need for good English and clear presentation in your answers.

Name: ....

Section A consists of multiple choice questions.

There are 20 marks available.
Answer all questions.

For each question you should shade in **one** box.

An example is shown below.

Which food is high in fat?

A Bread

B Cheese

C Broccoli

D Apple

Practice Exam Paper 2

Question 1 is about diet, nutrition and health.

0 1 · 1 Which mineral element is needed by the body to assist with the absorption of Vitamin C?

    A Fluoride ◯

    B Calcium ◯

    C Phosphorous ◯

    D Iron ◯   **[1 mark]**

0 1 · 2 High blood pressure can be linked to a diet high in:

    A Sugar ◯

    B Protein ◯

    C Calcium ◯

    D Salt ◯   **[1 mark]**

0 1 · 3 A deficiency of vitamin B12 is linked to which condition?

    A Heart disease ◯

    B Pernicious anaemia ◯

    C Spina bifida ◯

    D Stroke ◯   **[1 mark]**

0 1 · 4 Folate (folic acid) is needed both before and during early pregnancy for the development of what in the foetus?

    A Strong bones ◯

    B The neural tube ◯

    C The liver ◯

    D Blood ◯   **[1 mark]**

Question 2 is about food safety.

0 2 · 1 Food poisoning is most likely to occur if:

    A   cooked meat is stored in the refrigerator. ◯

    B   cold cooked meat is stored in the freezer. ◯

    C   food is stored above 63°C for no more than two hours. ◯

    D   cooked meat is kept at room temperature. ◯   **[1 mark]**

0 2 · 2 Ambient food storage areas should be:

    A   warm, dark and pest-proof. ◯

    B   damp, cool and well ventilated. ◯

    C   light, warm and secure. ◯

    D   dry, cool and well ventilated. ◯   **[1 mark]**

0 2 · 3 If cooked food is not chilled quickly:

    A   viruses will produce toxins. ◯

    B   moulds will begin to grow. ◯

    C   bacteria will start to multiply. ◯

    D   allergens will be created. ◯   **[1 mark]**

0 2 · 4 Which colour board should raw chicken be prepared upon?

    A   Blue ◯

    B   Brown ◯

    C   Red ◯

    D   Green ◯   **[1 mark]**

Practice Exam Paper 2

Question 3 is about food science.

0 3 . 1 Which type of sugar is most effective when aerating a cream cake mixture?

A Demerara sugar   ◯

B Caster sugar   ◯

C Icing sugar   ◯

D Dark molasses   ◯   **[1 mark]**

0 3 . 2 Eggs are cooked in a soufflé. How does heat change the raw egg proteins?

A The eggs are gelatinised.   ◯

B The eggs are fermented.   ◯

C The eggs are coagulated.   ◯

D The eggs are melted.   ◯   **[1 mark]**

0 3 . 3 Which heat transfer method is most likely to bring about dextrinisation?

A Microwave rays   ◯

B Convection currents   ◯

C Conduction   ◯

D Radiated heat   ◯   **[1 mark]**

0 3 . 4 When a blow torch is used on the surface of a crème brûlée, how is the sugar affected?

A It is condensed.   ◯

B It is coagulated.   ◯

C It is caramelised.   ◯

D It is curdled.   ◯   **[1 mark]**

Question 4 is about food provenance.

0 4 · 1 Which of the following is a way of reducing food waste?

    A FIFO (Fridge Intensive Food Organisation) ◯

    B FIFO (Food In Fridge Organisation) ◯

    C FIFO (First In First Out) ◯

    D FIFO (Food In Foil Opened) ◯   **[1 mark]**

0 4 · 2 What is hydroponic farming?

    A Fish farms which allow newly hatched young to mature before releasing them into the wild. ◯

    B Farms where fruits and vegetables are grown using large irrigation channels. ◯

    C Farms where fruit and vegetables are grown using large spray-armed sprinkler systems. ◯

    D Fruits and vegetables grown in large polytunnels using nutrient-rich liquids rather than soil. ◯   **[1 mark]**

0 4 · 3 MSC is an international non-profit organisation with a mission to stop overfishing. What does MSC stand for?

    A More Sustainable Catches ◯

    B Marine Sourced Cod ◯

    C Marine Sustainable Catches ◯

    D Marine Stewardship Council ◯   **[1 mark]**

0 4 · 4 What is the primary process that turns wheat into flour called?

    A Crushing ◯

    B Milling ◯

    C Grinding ◯

    D Rolling ◯   **[1 mark]**

Practice Exam Paper 2

Question 5 is about food choices.

0 5 . 1 People who have an adverse reaction to gluten are described as:

A diabetic ◯

B lactose intolerant ◯

C anaemic ◯

D coeliac ◯ **[1 mark]**

0 5 . 2 Salt in the diet can be linked to high blood pressure. What is the recommended amount per day for adults?

A No more than 10g. ◯

B No more than 12g. ◯

C No more than 6g. ◯

D No more than 8g. ◯ **[1 mark]**

0 5 . 3 A baby is born with a supply of iron in which organ of the body?

A Liver ◯

B Kidneys ◯

C Spleen ◯

D Blood ◯ **[1 mark]**

0 5 . 4 Which of the following is NOT a type of carbohydrate?

A Starch ◯

B Sucrose ◯

C Glycogen ◯

D Cholesterol ◯ **[1 mark]**

Section B

Answer all questions in this section.
There are 80 marks available.

Question 6 is about diet, nutrition and health.

0 6 · 1 Kiwi fruit is a good source of vitamin C, which could be included in a fresh fruit salad. Name two other good sources of vitamin C that could be included in a fresh fruit salad.

....

[2 marks]

0 6 · 2 State four reasons why the body requires vitamin C.

....

....

....

....

[4 marks]

0 6 · 3 Vitamin C is a water-soluble vitamin that is easily lost in food preparation. Give four ways to help prevent the loss of vitamin C.

....

....

....

....

[4 marks]

0 6 . 4 Discuss the advantages and disadvantages of buying fruits and vegetables grown in the UK.

[6 marks]

Question 7 is about functional and chemical properties of protein.

0 7 . 1 Explain how using an electric whisk to make meringue changes the protein structure of egg white. You may use diagrams to support your answer.

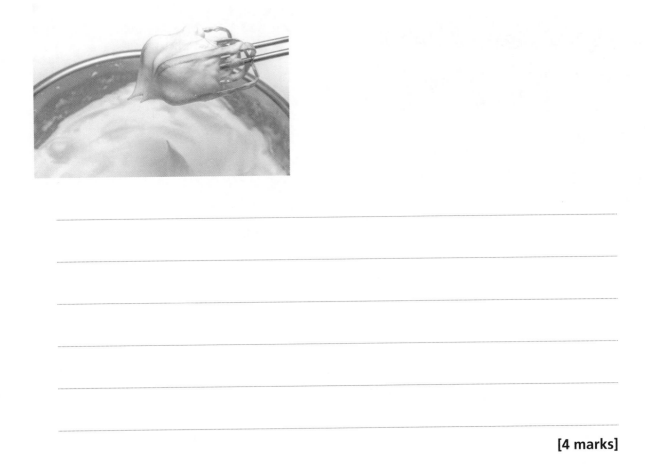

....

....

....

....

....

....

[4 marks]

0 7 · 2 Explain the scientific reasons for the changes that occur when eggs are boiled.

....

....

....

....

....

....

[6 marks]

0 7 . 3 Explain why milk curdles when lemon juice is added.

[6 marks]

Practice Exam Paper 2

Question 8 is about cooking food, heat transfer and selecting appropriate cooking methods.

0 8 · 1 Describe how heat transfer methods work when boiling potatoes on the hob.

....

[2 marks]

0 8 · 2 Steaming is classed as a water-based method of cooking. Name two other classifications of cooking methods, giving an example for each of a dish or recipe cooked in that way.

....

....

[4 marks]

0 8 · 3 State two health benefits from choosing to steam vegetables.

....

....

[2 marks]

0 8 · 4 Using data from the chart below, explain how cooking methods affect the nutritional outcome of potatoes cooked in different ways.

Potatoes cooked in different ways	Vitamin C content per 100g portion	Fat content per 100g portion
Potatoes boiled in water	6 mg	0.1 g
Oven chips baked	12 mg	4.9 g
Potato crisps	35 mg	28.8 mg

Source: Manual of Nutrition 12th edition

....

....

....

....

....

[6 marks]

Question 9 is about food safety.

0 9 · 1 'High-risk foods are most likely to cause food poisoning.'

Explain this statement.

[6 marks]

0 9 · 2 Explain how a temperature probe should be used correctly on a cooked chicken.

[4 marks]

Question 10 is about food production.

10.1 Name two types of milk that have been processed to have a longer shelf life than fresh milk.

[2 marks]

10.2 Explain the differences between skimmed and semi-skimmed milk.

[2 marks]

The picture shows a refrigerator stocked with alternatives to cows' milk.

10.3 Give four examples of what these products can be made from.

[4 marks]

`1 0 . 4` Explain why cows' milk alternatives have become very popular in the last few years.

....

....

....

....

....

[4 marks]

Question 11 is about provenance and sustainability.

11·1 Explain what is meant by free-range farming.

_____

_____

[1 mark]

11·2 What are the benefits of free-range farming?

_____

_____

[3 marks]

11·3 Give two examples of free-range products.

_____

[2 marks]

11·4 Explain what it means if chicken has a label which says it has been 'barn reared'.

_____

_____

_____

[3 marks]

11·5 Explain how organic vegetables and fruits are grown.

_____

_____

_____

[3 marks]

END OF QUESTIONS

Answers

Food Preparation Skills – pages 148–152

Page 148 Knife Skills

1. c) ✓ [1]
2. d) ✓ [1]
3. **Three from: Safety Rule:** A flat and stable surface should be used for cutting **[1] Reason:** to prevent slipping and movement/injury. **[1] Safety Rule:** Keep knives sharp and clean **[1] Reason:** a blunt knife is more likely to cause a cut because more pressure needs to be applied to use it to cut. **[1] Safety Rule:** Keep knife handles grease-free **[1] Reason:** so that they do not slip and cause injury. **[1] Safety Rule:** Hold the point downwards when carrying a knife **[1] Reason:** to protect others in the room. **[1] Safety Rule:** Do not put knives in the washing-up bowl **[1] Reason:** someone may put their hand in the bowl and sustain a cut **[1] Safety Rule:** Do not leave a knife on the edge of a table or chopping board **[1] Reason:** this can fall and cause injury. **[1]**
4. **Name of knife hold 1:** Bridge hold **[1] Explanation:** Form a bridge with thumb and index finger, hold item flat side down on chopping board, position knife under the bridge and cut firmly downwards. **[1] Name of knife hold 2:** Claw grip **[1] Explanation:** Place item to be cut flat side down on chopping board, shape hand into a claw, tuck thumb inside fingers, rest the claw on item to be sliced, use other hand to slice the item, moving clawed fingers away as cutting progresses. **[1]**

Page 149 Fish

1. c) ✓ [1]
2. d) ✓ [1]
3. Fish cooks quickly because the **muscle [1]** is short and the **connective tissue [1]** is thin. The connective tissue is made up of **collagen [1]** and will change into **gelatine [1]** and **coagulate [1]** at **60 °C [1]**.
4. a) Flat fish [1]
   b) **Any flat fish, e.g.** Plaice; Sole; Halibut [1]
   c) Filleting knife [1]
   d) Blue [1]
   e) Use a filleting knife to descale and remove the fins. Cut off the head just behind the gills. **[1]** Cut from head to tail down to the bone, to one side of the centre line. **[1]** Turn the knife almost parallel to the table. Make a long, smooth cut horizontally against the backbone towards the outer edge. Separate the fillet from the bone and remove it. **[1]**

Page 150 Meat

1. d) ✓ [1]
2. c) ✓ [1]
3. Muscles that work a lot, such as the thighs and shoulders of animals, give tough meat, e.g. shin beef, brisket. **[1]** Cuts of meat from muscle areas that do a lot of work will need longer, slower cooking methods in wet heat, e.g. stewing, braising, pot roasting and casseroling. **[1]** Meat from tougher cuts can be ground or minced to break up the connective tissues so that it cooks more quickly. **[1]**
4. Red [1]
5. **Any two of:** Using a marinade **[1]**; Mincing **[1]**; Using a steak hammer **[1]**
6. The **browning [1]** of meat is caused by a reaction with natural **sugars [1]** and proteins to produce a dark colour. This occurrence is called the **Maillard [1]** reaction or non-enzymic browning. As the meat cooks, the proteins **coagulate [1]** and produce a firm texture. Collagen is broken down into **gelatine [1]**.

Page 151 Prepare, Combine and Shape

1. a) ✓ [1]
2. Folding and stirring are methods used to **combine [1]** and **mix [1]** ingredients. Folding is different to stirring because it is a careful **figure-of-eight [1]** movement used for adding flour when **cake [1]** making. Folding **retains [1]** air in a cake mixture helping the cooked cake to have a light airy **texture [1]**.
3. a) Rolling pin **[1]**
   b) Roll **[1]** and fold **[1]**
   c) Piping bag **[1]**; Star nozzle **[1]**
   d) Portion **[1]**, roll **[1]** and tie by hand **[1]**

Page 152 Dough

1. a) By using a pasta machine (or rolling pin). [1]
   b) The texture changes **[1]** to hard and dry. **[1]**
2. b) ✓ [1]
3. **Any two valid ingredients with correct colours achieved for [4], e.g.** Beetroot powder **[1]** – purple **[1]**; Spinach powder **[1]** – green **[1]**; Tomato puree **[1]** – red **[1]**; Squid ink **[1]** – black **[1]**
4. Pastry; Bread; Pasta **circled [3]**
5. The fat is melted **[1]**, the water and fat are heated to a rolling boil **[1]** then mixed into the flour. [1]
6. True [1]

Food Nutrition and Health – pages 153–158

Page 153 Protein and Fat

1. amino acids [2]
2. a) **Any three from:** Soya; Nuts; Seeds; Pulses (lentils, kidney beans etc.); Mycoprotein (Quorn); TVP (Texturised Vegetable protein) [3]
   b) Cauliflower cheese; Mushroom and Lentil Bake **circled.** [2]
3. When proteins of low biological value (LBV) are eaten together to provide all essential amino acids. **[1] Examples:** beans on toast, lentil soup and bread, hummus and pitta bread etc. **[1]**
4. fatty acids **[1]** glycerol **[1]**
5. c) ✓ [1]
6. **Any three suitable answers, e.g.** Oily fish; Nuts; Seeds; Avocados; Vegetable oils; Soya beans; Some functional food such as yoghurts and spreads (e.g. Activia, Benecol) [3]

Page 154 Carbohydrate

1. energy [1]
2. Photosynthesis [1]
3. Constipation is when faeces become difficult to expel from the body **[1]** because they are hard and small. **[1]**
4. c) ✓ [1]
5. Monosaccharides, Disaccharides, Polysaccharides [3]
6. Starches have to be digested into sugars **[1]** before they can be absorbed into the bloodstream. **[1]** This is slow energy release.
7. Excess carbohydrate is converted into fat and stored under the skin. **[1]** This is the main cause of obesity, which can be directly linked to many conditions such as heart disease, stroke, cancers and Type 2 diabetes. **[1]** In addition, a high consumption of sugar in the diet in the main cause of dental decay. **[1]**

Page 155 Vitamins

1. **Three from:** Oranges; Lemons; Limes; Grapefruit; Kiwi fruit; Blackcurrants; Potatoes; Tomatoes; Green vegetables, e.g. kale, cabbage, Brussel sprouts [3]
2. b) ✓ [1]
3. Folate (Folic acid) [1]
4. **Three from:** Prepare foods quickly just before serving; Use small amounts of boiling water to cook; Use cooking liquid to make sauces/gravy; Avoid lots of cutting of vegetables; Instead of cooking in water, steam, fry or grill. [3]
5. **Any suitable function given for each vitamin. Examples given in the table.** [5]

Vitamin	Function
Vitamin A	Normal iron metabolism; Maintenance of normal vision; Maintenance of skin and membranes; Healthy immune function
Vitamin K	Normal clotting of blood
Vitamin C	Absorption of iron; Production of collagen to bind connective tissue; Antioxidant – protects from environmental pollutants
Vitamin D	Absorption of calcium and phosphorus; Maintenance and strength of bones and teeth
Vitamin B1	Release of energy from carbohydrates; Healthy nervous system function; Normal growth in children

Page 156 Minerals and Water

1. Iron [1]
2. Iron supports the production of **haemoglobin [1]** in red blood cells, which transport **oxygen [1]** around the body.
3. a) Dehydration [1]
   b) **Any three from:** For normal brain function; To decrease risk of kidney problems; For normal blood pressure; To assist healthy bowel movements; To make body fluids – blood saliva mucus membranes; To aid milk production in lactating women. [3]
4. a) Rickets [1]
   b) Osteoporosis [1]
5. **Three from:** Red meats; Liver; Lentils; Dried apricots; Cocoa; Chocolate; Corned beef; Curry spices; Green leafy vegetables e.g. spinach; Breakfast cereals fortified with iron. [3]

Page 157 Making Informed Choices

1. Fruit and Vegetables (green); Potatoes, Bread, Rice Pasta and other starchy carbohydrates (yellow). [2]
2. For breast-fed babies, the first milk that a mother produces is called **colostrum [1]** and it is full of **antibodies. [1]**
3. Anaemia is caused by a lack of iron in the blood. After menstruation begins in puberty, [1] iron is needed in greater amounts to replace blood losses. [1]
4. Osteoporosis **underlined.** [1]
5. Pulse vegetables [1] and beans, such as lentils, soya beans, kidney beans, baked beans, chickpeas. [1]
6. Calcium [1] – The developing baby's bones require a good supply of calcium from the mother's diet. [1] Iron [1] – A pregnant woman will need an iron-rich diet to make additional blood for the baby and to lay down an iron store in the baby's liver. [1] Folate (folic acid) [1] – This is needed both before and during early

pregnancy for the development of the neural tube in the baby. This is to help prevent the condition spina bifida. [1]

Page 158 Diet, Nutrition and Health

1. Obesity [1]
2. Body Mass Index (BMI) [1]
3. Elderly people require a good supply of calcium and vitamin D in the diet to ensure maximum bone strength and help prevent the condition osteoporosis. [1] This can cause bones to become more brittle and break easily. It can also cause the spine to curve, making walking more difficult. [1]
4. Fibre/NSP [1]
5. Sugar increases acids on the teeth [1], which erode the protective enamel on the teeth causing irreparable tooth decay. [1]
6. **Any three from:** Tiredness; Lack of energy; Shortness of breath; Pale complexion [3]
7. In Type 2 **diabetes [1]** too little or no **insulin [1]** is produced in the **pancreas [1]** resulting in high levels of **sugar [1]** in the **blood. [1]**

Food Science – pages 159–163

Page 159 Cooking of Food, Heat Transfer and Selecting Appropriate Cooking Methods

1. **Oven-roasted vegetables – Any two from:** Browned; Crispy; Added fat [2]
   Boiled vegetables – Any two from: Tender/Soft; Wet; No added fat [2]
2. b) ✓ [1]
3. Radiation [1] from a grill. [1]
4. a) It tenderises the salmon [1] and makes it safe to eat. [1]
   b) Marinating adds flavour and/or colour. [1] It tenderises the chicken. [1]
5. When making a sauce, heat is transferred from the hob through the base of the pan by **conduction [1]** and through the sauce by **convection. [1]** Stirring prevents **sticking [1]** on the base of the pan and distributes **heat [1]** to aid **thickening. [1]**

Page 160 Proteins and Enzymic Browning

1. a) Once cut, the fruit inside the skin allows oxidation/air. [1] This is enzymic browning. [1]
   b) **Any one from:** Add lemon juice; Poach them; Add a glaze [1]
2. a) It will be set. [1] It will be browned. [1]
   b) The heat [1] causes the mixture to coagulate. [1] Coagulation is a type of protein denaturation [1], which occurs when the amino acids found in the egg protein change shape after cooking. [1]
3. a) Bromelain [1]
   b) It would tenderise the prawns. [1]
4. b) ✓ [1] c) ✓ [1]
5. Gluten **circled.** [1]

Page 161 Carbohydrates

1. It softens the onions. [1] It sweetens the onions. [1] It caramelises the sugars in the onions. [1]
2. a) **Any two from:** Cornflour; Plain wheatflour; Arrowroot; Thickening granules [2]
   b) Starch gelatinises in moist heat. [1] The starch swells and thickens when boiled. [1] It needs stirring. [1]
3. **Any two from:** Texture becomes crisp/crunchy; Flavour becomes sweeter; Colour changes to charred/golden. [2]
4. a) For heat transfer distribution [1]; For distribution of starch in the flour [1]; Smooth gelatinisation/no lumps [1]; To prevent sticking to the base of the pan. [1]
   b) ii) ✓ [1] iv) ✓ [1]

Page 162 Fats and Oils

1. To provide colour (yellow colour) [1], to add a buttery flavour [1], shortening [1] due to preventing the development of gluten [1] in the flour dough.
2. a) **See middle column of table below.** [3]
   b) **See last column of table below. Any correct dish for each preparation method, examples given in the table.** [3]

Temperature of Fat	Food Preparation Method	Example of Dish
Chilled temperature	Rubbing-in	Shortcrust pastry
Room temperature	Creaming	Bakewell tart toppings
Warm pan temperature	Melting method	Flapjack

3. a) **Two from:** To create a light cake; To create an open/fluffy texture; So the cake rises. [2]
   b) **Any two from:** Creaming method; Whisking method; Using a food mixer [2]
4. Air-in-fat [1]

Page 163 Raising Agents

1. a) **Any two suitable recipes/products [2] with appropriate mechanical method of trapping air [2]. Examples given in the table.** [4]

Recipe/Product Name	Mechanical (Physical) Method to Trap Air
Puff pastry	Folding/Layering
Cakes	Sieving flour/Beating
Cream	Whipping to thicken
Swiss roll	Whisking

   b) Chemical [1], **Example:** Baking powder/Self-raising flour/Bicarbonate of soda/Cream of tartar [1] OR **Biological [1]**, **Example:** Yeast [1]

2.

Product	Raising Agent
Victoria Sandwich	S.R. flour [1]
Muffins	Baking powder [1]
English pancakes	Beating [1]
Choux buns	Steam production [1]

3. Bicarbonate of soda [1]
4. Gas-in-liquid foam [1]
5. A ready-mix raising agent [1] in the correct proportion [1] of cream of tartar [1] and bicarbonate of soda. [1]

Food Safety – pages 164–168

Page 164 Microorganisms, Enzymes and Food Spoilage

1. **Two from:** Bacteria; Yeast; Mould; Fungi/fungus [2]
2. **Three from:** Food; Temperature/warmth; Moisture/liquid; pH value; Time; HBV protein content; Oxygen/air; Carbon dioxide (Do **not** accept a named method of preservation). [3]
3. **Three from:** Change in colour/discolouration; Change in size/it shrinks; Change in texture/soft/dry/slimy; Change in consistency; Mould; Unpleasant smell; Unpleasant taste. [3]
4. **Three from:** Make sure storage containers are clean; Store dry foods in airtight containers/sealed packets; Store in a cool, dry place; Wash shelves regularly/deal with spills; Do not top up existing stock with new; Check storage times/best before dates; Cupboards should be free from vermin and pests.[3]
5. **Two from:** Add lemon juice to fruit to prevent browning; Blanche vegetables before freezing; Immerse potatoes in water to prevent discolouration; Refrigerate or freeze; Dehydrate [2]

Page 165 Microorganisms in Food Production

1. Bacteria are **single**-celled [1] organisms which are able to reproduce **rapidly.** [1] Some are **harmful** [1] and cause **food poisoning** [1] or even death. Some are harmless and used in **cheese**-making. [1] **Probiotic** [1] bacteria help **digestion.** [1]
2. a) In blue-veined cheeses, e.g. Stilton, Danish blue, harmless moulds are used to produce specific flavours, textures and aromas. [1] Some sausages, such as salami, incorporate starter cultures of moulds to improve flavour and reduce bacterial spoilage during curing. [1] Microbial rennet is used for making vegetarian and other cheeses. [1] Mould can improve the appearance of foods. [1]
   b) Cheese and yoghurt manufacture uses cultures of lactic acid bacteria [1] to produce characteristic flavours and textures to these products. [1] Fermented foods e.g. Sauerkraut: bacteria will improve flavour and texture [1] and have a positive effect on the bacteria flora of the digestive gut. [1]

3. **Three from:** Pepperoni; Chorizo; Salami; Dried ham [3]

Page 166 Bacterial Contamination

1.

Name of Bacteria	One Food Source	One Symptom
E-Coli	**One from:** Raw meat; Untreated milk; Water [1]	**One from:** Vomiting; Blood in diarrhoea; Kidney damage or failure; Gastroenteritis in humans [1]
Campylobacter	**One from:** Meat; Shellfish; Untreated water; Washing raw poultry [1]	**One from:** Diarrhoea; Headache; Fever; Abdominal pain (**Do not accept** vomiting) [1]
Bacillus Cereus	**One from:** Cooked rice; Herbs and spices; Starchy food products [1]	**One from:** Nausea; Vomiting; Diarrhoea [1]
Staphylococcus Aureus	**One from:** Anything touched by dirty hands; Cooked sliced meats; Dairy products [1]	**One from:** Vomiting; Diarrhoea; Abdominal pain [1]

2. Food-poisoning bacteria is caused by bacteria multiplying in or on food products. [1] Food-borne disease is caused by pathogens carried on food – they do not multiply on the food but in a person who has eaten the food. [1]
3. **Three from:** Moisture/moist/damp; Oxygen; Time; Warmth/warm; Food [3]

Page 167 Buying and Storing Food

1. **Answers could include the following points for a maximum of [4]. Answers must relate to food handling and storage:** Food poisoning occurs when foods spoil rapidly [1] because of a high-water content and high nutritional content. [1] Because of warm, moist conditions [1] food poisoning would occur in **any named high-risk food** [1] (e.g. raw and cooked meat, poultry and fish, cheese, milk and dairy products, eggs and cooked rice). Food deteriorates rapidly making it unsafe [1] to eat because of microorganism/enzyme/natural decay activity. [1] When using highly perishable food, handlers must check date marks [1] so that safety of handled products is ensured due to their short shelf life. [1] Cross-contamination [1] will occur if high risk foods are exposed to poor hygiene or storage: **any of the named following examples:** food to food (raw/cooked/ pre purchased)/ Personal or kitchen hygiene/Food handler to food/Equipment to food/Pest to food/Pet to food. [1] Store at correct temperatures/out of the danger zone. [1]

2. **Any two rules from the following [2] with correct explanation as shown below [2]:**

Food Safety Rule	Explanation
• Store correctly as soon as possible.	• To slow down microbial growth/deterioration/spoilage.
• Do not leave at room temperature/in the danger zone.	• Bacteria multiply more rapidly at warm temperatures; Bacteria multiply rapidly between 5°C and 63°C/danger zone; Bacteria multiply every 20 minutes.
• Store at 0 to below 5°C; Store in the refrigerator, NOT on lower shelf; Store in the freezer –18°C.	• Bacteria multiply slowly in cold temperatures; Bacteria are dormant in the freezer; To prevent pathogenic bacteria multiplying they must be stored below 5°C; Fish should be not stored in the danger zone (5–63°C).
• Cover in airtight container.	• Covering prevents cross contamination.
• Use by the use-by date.	• Use-by dates indicate when the food is still safe to eat.
• Use oldest food first; Label clearly with date.	• Allows for stock rotation; First in first out (FIFO).
• Check internal temperature of the refrigerator.	• The refrigerator must be working correctly and be well maintained.

3. d) ✓ [1]

Page 168 Preparing and Cooking Food

1. **Four from:** Tie back hair; Cover long hair/beards with hair nets; Do not cough, spit, pick nose or sneeze over foods; Do not chew when serving food; Do not put fingers into food being served; Use clean teaspoon each time for tasting foods; Do not double dip when tasting food; Wear protective clothing, e.g. clean apron; Wear disposable gloves when handling food; Wash hands before serving food; Wash hands after using the toilet, on return from outside and after handling raw foods; Keep fingernails short and clean; Do not wear nail varnish or false nails; Do not allow sweat to go onto food; Use tongs and other utensils not fingers; Do not lick fingers or cooking utensils; Use blue gloves when handling different types of food, e.g. cooked, and raw; Cover any cuts with a protective, waterproof, blue/bright-coloured plaster; Do not wear jewellery; Do not serve food if suffering from illness, sickness, diarrhoea or fever; any other relevant response. **[4]**
2. Cooked meat **[1] Plus two from:** Poultry/cook chill products; Cooked rice; Gravies, stocks, soups and stews; Ice cream; Dairy foods; Named products containing fresh cream; Pâté; Pre-packed sandwiches; Protein-based baby foods; Fish; Raw egg, e.g. in chilled desserts and mayonnaise; Shellfish and seafood / named shellfish or seafood; Soya milk; Unwashed fruit and vegetables. **[2]**
3. **One from:** Digital probe; Food probe; Food thermometer; Meat probe; Meat thermometer; Temperature probe (Do **not** accept just thermometer or probe) **[1]**
4. c) ✓ **[1]**

Food Choices – pages 169–173

Page 169 Food Choices

1. Kosher meat **[1]**
2. Anaphylaxis **underlined** **[1]**
3. Coeliac disease is a condition where people have an adverse reaction to gluten **[1]**, a protein found in wheat, barley, rye, and – to a lesser extent – oats. **[1]** Coeliacs cannot absorb any nutrients if they eat gluten and this can cause severe pain, anaemia and malnutrition. **[1]**
4. Lactose intolerance **[1]**
5. Gluten free – the symbol from Coeliac UK. **[1]**
6.

Religion	Dietary Restriction
Islam **[1]**	No pork
	Only Halal meat
Hinduism **[1]**	No beef or beef products
Christianity **[1]**	No particular dietary restrictions

7. Type 1 usually occurs in childhood and is not associated with excess sugar in the diet or obesity. **[1]** Type 2 generally occurs in adults over 40. **[1]** 90% of people with diabetes have this type. It is linked to obesity and those that have a high sugar diet. **[1]** Both types are controlled with insulin.

Page 170 British and International Cuisines

1. b) ✓ **[1]**
2. Cheddar **[1]**
3.

Country	Dishes	Key Ingredients and Flavours
England	Cornish pasty **[1]**;	A folded pastry with filling (meat, vegetable, cheese) **[1]**;
	Shepherd's pie **[1]**	A layer of meat sauce with mashed potato on top **[1]**
France	Bouillabaisse **[1]**;	Fish soup **[1]**;
	Tarte tatin **[1]**	Sweet apple pie with pastry at bottom **[1]**
Spain	Tortilla **[1]**;	Egg omelette filled with fried potatoes and onion **[1]**;
	Paella **[1]**	Rice with seafood **[1]**
Italy	Minestrone **[1]**;	Soup with small pasta **[1]**;
	Lasagne **[1]**	Layers of pasta and meat/vegetables with white sauce on top **[1]**

4. It is the testing of two similar products. **[1]** There are three samples but two are the same. **[1]** All samples are coded differently. **[1]** The aim is to try and identify the odd one out. **[1]**
5. b) ✓ **[1]**

Page 171 Sensory Evaluation

1. Sensory **analysis [1]** involves using our **five [1]** senses to **evaluate [1]** how much we **like [1]** a dish. We use these senses **together [1]** when we **eat [1]** our food.
2. Taste **[1]** Sight **[1]** Smell/Aroma **[1]** Touch **[1]** Hearing **[1]**
3. Find a quiet area. **[1]** Invite people to taste. **[1]** Provide water to cleanse the palate. **[1]** Code the food samples. **[1]** Use a recording sheet. **[1]** Clean eating implements if required. **[1]**

Page 172 Food Labelling

1. a) ✓ **[1]**
2. Guideline daily amounts **[1]**
3. In descending order with the greatest amount first. **[1]**
4. **Six from:** Name of the product; Weight or volume; Allergen information; Date mark; Storage instructions; Cooking instructions – to ensure the food is safe to eat; Place of origin; Name and address of manufacturer; Batch mark for traceability; Nutritional information on pre-packaged foods **[6]**
5. They must be clearly highlighted in bold or underlined.**[1]** They must be clearly identifiable by the consumer. **[1]**

Page 173 Factors Affecting Food Choice

1. Our enjoyment of food is affected by what the food **looks, [1]** smells **[1]** and tastes **[1]** like.
2. **Any three suitable answers. Examples include:** Christianity – Christmas – Christmas Cake, Christmas Pudding etc; Judaism – Passover – Unleavened bread, Hanukkah, brisket, latkes chicken soup; Islam – Eid – dates eaten to break the fast, al-ache mutton/lamb-based dishes. **[3]**
3. Food is fresher **[1]**; Minimal food miles reducing carbon footprint **[1]**; Supporting local business **[1]**.
4. imported **[1]**
5. **Answer to include discussion relating to:** Special offers; Product placement in the store; In-store promotions; Advertising; Money-off coupons; Recipe cards. **[3]**

Food Provenance – pages 174–178

Page 174 Food and the Environment

1. **Any two suitable answers, for example:** Rissoles **[1]**; Bubble and squeak **[1]**; Soup **[1]**; Corned beef hash **[1]**
2. c) ✓ **[1]**
3. b) ✓ **[1]**
4. Earthworms **[1]** Food waste **[1]**
5. Wise shopping and planning ahead reduces the amount of food bought in the first place **[1]**; FIFO (first-in first-out storage) reduces food wasted **[1]**; Only prepare the food you actually need, so nothing is needlessly thrown

away **[1]**; Use food before it goes out of date, so that food does not have to be thrown away for safety reasons **[1]**; Use leftover food to make other dishes, thereby avoiding having to throw leftover food out **[1]**; Do home composting so that any food you have to throw out does not have to be transported to a landfill site **[1]**.

Page 175 Food Provenance and Production Methods

1. c) ✓ **[1]**
2. Foods produced using nutrient rich liquids instead of soil. **[1]** Takes place in vast polytunnels or greenhouses **[1]** with controlled environments **[1]**. Expensive so only for high end crops. **[1]**
3. b) ✓ **[1]** c) ✓ **[1]**
4. **Five from:** Manufacturer **[1]**; Producer or grower **[1]**; Distributer **[1]**; Transporter **[1]**; Retailer **[1]**; Consumer **[1]**
5. **Any three from:** Fewer small farm communities; A greater number of larger business farms; Large numbers of animals and poultry being kept in massive buildings; and fed on high nutrient feeds in a short period of time, designed to maximise growth; Widespread use of antibiotics, growth enhancers, fertilisers and pesticides; Small farm fields being opened up/woodland destroyed to make room for large machinery access. **[3]**

Page 176 Sustainability of Food

1. b) ✓ **[1]**
2. True **[1]**
3. a) **Any two from**: The Fairtrade logo means that the farmer in a developing country who produced the goods gets a realistic income **[1]**; Investment in the local community takes place **[1]**; There are better working conditions for the producing farmer **[1]**; A fair price is paid for the goods **[1]**; Sustainable production methods are used **[1]**.
   b) Possible answers, **any two from**: Chocolate; Tea; Coffee; Bananas **(two answers needed for 1 mark)**.
4. The Red Tractor logo tells us that the food has been produced, processed and packed to the Red Tractor standards **[1]**; The flag on the Red Tractor logo shows the country of origin **[1]**; Red Tractor labelling assures good standards of food hygiene and safety **[1]**; Red Tractor labelling assures high standards of equipment used in production **[1]**; Red Tractor assures good standards of animal health and welfare **[1]**; Environmental issues are respected by Red Tractor suppliers **[1]**; Red Tractor standards ensure responsible use of pesticides **[1]**. Any product with the Red Tractor logo can be traced from farm to fork **[1]**.

Page 177 Food Production

1. Evaporated milk that has sugar added and is very thick. **[1]**
2. **Three from:** Single **[1]**; Whipping **[1]**; Double **[1]**; Extra thick **[1]**
3. a) **Any three suitable answers, e.g. three from:** Red Leicester **[1]**; Cheddar **[1]**; Cheshire **[1]**; Lancashire **[1]**; Wensleydale **[1]**; Stilton **[1]**; Caerphilly **[1]**
   b) **Any three suitable answers, e.g. three from**: Brie **[1]**; Camembert **[1]**; Fromage frais **[1]**; Roquefort **[1]**; Saint Agur **[1]**.
4. Durum wheat **[1]**
5. a) Bran **[1]**
   b) White flour **[1]**
6. Lactose intolerant **[1]** people can substitute animal milk in their diet with milk made from soya, rice, coconut, almond or oats. These milks don't contain lactose. **[1]** Vegans **[1]** won't drink milk from an animal. Veganism seeks to avoid causing suffering and pain to animals but it also seeks to avoid their exploitation when it comes to animal-based milks. **[1]**

Page 178 Food Processing

1. **Four from:** Sunlight **[1]**; Oven drying **[1]**; Roller drying **[1]**; Spray drying **[1]**; AFD/Accelerated freeze drying **[1]**
2. a) Milk is heated to 140 degrees for 5 seconds then put into an airtight container. **[1]** It can then be stored for up to 6 months. **[1]**
   b) Ultra heat treated **[1]**
   c) Slight change in taste **[1]**; Colour remains similar **[1]**; Little change in nutrients **[1]**
3. a) Strictly controlled X-rays are passed through the food **[1]** which delays ripening. **[1]**
   b) Vitamin A **[1]**, Vitamin C **[1]**, Vitamin E **[1]**, Vitamin K **[1]** may be lost
   c) Food looks fresh **[1]** and tastes the same **[1]**

Pages 179–195 Practice Exam Paper 1

Section A

1.1 B		**[1]**
1.2 C		**[1]**
1.3 A		**[1]**
1.4 C		**[1]**
2.1 C		**[1]**
2.2 D		**[1]**
2.3 C		**[1]**
2.4 C		**[1]**
3.1 A		**[1]**
3.2 B		**[1]**
3.3 D		**[1]**
3.4 A		**[1]**
4.1 C		**[1]**
4.2 C		**[1]**
4.3 A		**[1]**
4.4 B		**[1]**
5.1 C		**[1]**
5.2 D		**[1]**
5.3 A		**[1]**
5.4 D		**[1]**

Section B

6.1 To consume the correct nutrients **[1]**; To consume nutrients in the right proportions **[1]**; To maintain a healthy weight (correct BMI) **[1]**; To reduce the risk of diet related disease or named disease (e.g. Type 2 diabetes, heart disease) **[1]**
6.2 **Three from:** Lack of knowledge of food **[1]**; Lack of food preparation skills/those with no skills relying on ready meals or takeaways **[1]**; Financial issues **[1]**; Lack of time to plan, shop and cook **[1]**; Family habits, preferences and routines about food **[1]**; Allergies and intolerances e.g. lactose intolerance **[1]**
6.3 **Ten from:** Plenty of calcium and vitamin D for her own and baby's bone and tooth development/named good sources of calcium and vitamin D, e.g. dairy products **[1]**; Look for fortified foods, e.g. breakfast cereals **[1]**; Consider methods of cooking in order to retain vital nutrients especially water soluble vitamins, e.g. steaming to retain vitamin C **[1]**; Drinks lots of water to prevent dehydration and help to provide a good milk supply when the baby is born **[1]**; Take folic acid (often as supplements) during pre- and early pregnancy to reduce risk of spina bifida **[1]**; Foods not recommended to be eaten in pregnancy include pâté, soft blue cheeses unless cooked, unpasteurised cheeses, with clear explanations linked to harmful bacteria particularly Listeria Monocytogenes **[1]**; Liver must be avoided because of the high vitamin A content/vitamin A supplements to be avoided **[1]**; Good supply of fruit and vegetables to provide fibre and vitamin C **[1]**; Healthy breakfast to avoid snacking **[1]**; Increase fibre to prevent constipation and haemorrhoids **[1]**; Iron-rich foods to prevent anaemia and for baby's developing blood supply – 3 months of iron are stored in a newborn baby's liver **[1]**; Not too many fatty and sugary foods **[1]**; Only in final three months of pregnancy, extra 200 calories needed per day **[1]**; Good protein supply for growth of the baby **[1]**; Important to follow dietary advice given by health professionals, particularly if mother has an underlying health condition **[1]**; Follow guidance on the Eatwell Guide **[1]**; Avoid alcohol **[1]**; Breastfeed to ensure mother–baby bond and to provide newborn baby with immunity benefits of mother's colostrum (first milk) **[1]**
7.1 **Four from:** Cook to gelatinise the starch (as all raw starch is indigestible) **[1]**; The hard foods become soft and safe to eat **[1]**; Cooking softens texture of potatoes **[1]**; Cooking swells rice and pasta by rehydration/

absorbing water [1]; Starch becomes digestible [1].

7.2 Sauce A has less starch in the roux so will give runnier sauce, therefore better to pour, [1] compared to Sauce B, which has more starch so will be a thicker sauce [1]. Starch gelatinises to thicken when it is heated to boiling. [1]

7.3 Sauce A should have a bigger viscosity circle [1] than Sauce B because it is runnier (less viscous). [1]

7.4

Preparation and cooking stages	Reasons
Peel old potatoes.	*To remove dirt and skin to speed up cooking.*
Chop potatoes.	To reduce size for quicker cooking. [1]
Boil potatoes.	To gelatinise starch and soften potato. [1]
Mash cooked potatoes.	To reduce volume, season and enable mixing with fish. [1]

7.5 Grilling is dry heat, radiated heat [1] that dextrinises potato starch [1], causing golden colour and crisp texture. [1]

8.1 Six from: The weight or volume (indicated by 'e', which stands for 'estimated weight' which allows for differences) [1]; Ingredients list from largest to smallest [1]; Allergen information in bold or highlighted [1]; Genetically Modified (GM) ingredients [1]; Date mark – use-by date or best-before date [1]; Storage instructions [1]; Cooking instructions (to ensure the food is safe to eat) [1]; Place of origin [1]; Batch mark for traceability [1]; E numbers – EU approved additives [1]; Nutritional information [1]

8.2 150ml milk; 125ml egg; 100g plain flour; 75g grated cheese; 60g chopped onion; 50g butter; 73ml water **[6 for all in correct order]**

8.3 In case of complaint. [1]

9.1 Two from: To make sure the food product meets the consumer's expectations [1]; To find out how a food product compares to similar ones on the market [1]; To check the quality of the product [1]; To ensure the consistency of the product [1]

9.2 The water cleanses the palate between each sample so that the flavours do not influence the results. [1]

9.3 Preference test would be used to see which product would be acceptable to the consumer [1]; The information gathered is very individual as it involves personal preference [1]; A large number of consumers need to be involved [1] to make the test reliable [1]

10.1 Select boiling as a cooking method [1] because pasta needs hydrating [1] to make it swell/become soft/cook [1]

10.2 Three from: To ensure even distribution of ingredients [1]; To prevent sticking [1]; To prevent burning/ browning [1]; To prevent lumps/ensure smooth texture [1]; To cook evenly [1]; To achieve the desired/correct consistency [1]; To allow for full gelatinisation/ thickening [1]

10.3 Grilling [1] because radiated heat browns food [1]

10.4 Four from: Oven-roasted vegetables are cooked in the oven in fat/oil [1]; Boiling only uses water [1]; Boiling does not brown the vegetables/Oven roasting browns the vegetables [1]; Boiling does not make the vegetables crispy/Oven roasting gives the vegetables a crispy outer [1]; Boiling gives a different flavour to the vegetables than oven roasting gives [1]

11.1 Two from: Support British farmers and the economy by buying local (farmers markets, local and regional producers) [1]; Eat more seasonal products (our bodies get the correct nutrients and trace elements that we need at the right time of year) [1]; Buy from suppliers nearer to Britain. [1]

11.2 Transportation around the world has meant that when local seasonal products are not available they can be imported all year round from hotter climates [1]. The transport used creates carbon dioxide gas (CO_2) [1] which is a contributor to global warming [1] and climate change [1]

12.1 There must be ability to track any food, feed, food-producing animal or substance that will be used for consumption. [1] It must be traced back to source [1] to quickly isolate the problem [1] and prevent contaminated products from reaching the customer. [1] All food handlers must have traceability information for suppliers and business [1] Retailers, including caterers, are not required to keep traceability information where they sell to the final consumer. However, where they supply food businesses, all traceability requirements must be adhered to. [1] They must have systems and procedures in place to allow for traceability. [1] Information to be made available to enforcement authorities on demand. [1] They must label or identify food placed on the market to facilitate its traceability. [1] Products of animal origin and sprouted seeds are subject to specific traceability requirements. [1]

Pages 196–212 Practice Exam Paper 2

Section A

1.1	D	[1]
1.2	D	[1]
1.3	B	[1]
1.4	B	[1]
2.1	D	[1]
2.2	D	[1]
2.3	C	[1]
2.4	C	[1]
3.1	B	[1]
3.2	C	[1]
3.3	D	[1]
3.4	C	[1]
4.1	C	[1]
4.2	D	[1]
4.3	D	[1]
4.4	B	[1]
5.1	D	[1]
5.2	C	[1]
5.3	A	[1]
5.4	D	[1]

Section B

6.1 Two from: Banana [1]; Blackberries [1]; Blackcurrants [1]; Blueberries [1]; Citrus fruit (or named example of citrus fruit) [1]; Cranberries [1]; Grapes [1]; Guava [1]; Loganberries [1]; Lychee [1]; Mango [1]; Melon [1]; Papaya [1]; Passionfruit [1]; Pineapple [1]; Strawberries [1]; Raspberries [1]

6.2 Four from: For the absorption of iron [1]; It is an antioxidant/to support the immune system [1]; To help prevent infection [1]; For healthy gums [1]; To help build strong bones and teeth [1]; To prevent scurvy [1]; To make connective tissue/for the formation of collagen [1]; For healthy skin [1]

6.3 Four from: Prepare food quickly just before serving [1]; Use small amounts of boiling water to cook [1]; Only add vegetables to boiling water to cook [1]; Use cooking liquid to make sauces and gravy [1]; Avoid lots of cutting of fruit and vegetables [1]; Tear vegetables rather than cut/use a very sharp knife [1]; Do not overcook vegetables [1]; Use the freshest vegetables possible [1]; Steam rather than boil [1]

6.4 Six from the following, but must include both advantages and disadvantages:
Advantages: Can be cheaper/saves money [1]; Can buy slightly imperfect products, saving waste – wonky vegetables [1]; Encourages use of seasonal British foods [1]; Fresher – greater vitamin content [1]; Less time in transit therefore fresher/better quality/better vitamin retention [1]; Easier to buy organic products/ reduced use of pesticides and chemical fertilisers [1]; Environmental considerations [1]; Reduced food miles/carbon footprint/pollution/

energy required to transport food [1]; Often considered to have a better flavour [1]; Supporting local economy/farmers/farm shops/farmers markets [1]; Pick your own farms can provide an educational and fun family activity. [1] **Disadvantages:** Climate – cannot grow certain crops, e.g. bananas, pineapples [1]; Limited variety/seasonally dependent [1]; Limited support for Fairtrade initiatives in developing countries [1]

7.1 Mechanical physical agitation breaks bonds [1] which uncoils the egg white protein [1]; Albumen foams [1] traps air and is denatured. The change is irreversible. [1] **Diagram may show uncoiling of protein, allowing air pockets.**

7.2 Heat causes denaturation of egg proteins [1] and coagulation [1] occurs as proteins clump and solidify [1]; Changes the appearance and texture of the food [1]; Protein sets due to the heat [1]; White coagulates at 60°C/yolk at 70°C [1]

7.3 Lemon juice is acid [1]; It has pH of 2 [1]; Causes clumping of proteins in milk (lactoglobulin, lactalbumen) [1] Curdling occurs [1]; Whey is squeezed out [1]; Denatured protein by acid conditions [1]

8.1 Conduction through the pan base [1]; Convection in the water [1]

8.2 Dry method [1]; Fat-based method [1]; **Any appropriate dishes/recipes cooked each way [2]**

8.3 No added fat [1]; Conserve water soluble nutrients [1]

8.4 [1] **(up to maximum of [3]) per correct use of data in each different cooking method. [1] (up to a maximum of [3])**

per accurate comparison, e.g. amount of fat added by the method; Vitamin C loss into water; Water soluble vitamin C retained by fat-based method.

9.1 High-risk foods are easily contaminated by bacteria [1] and so can cause food poisoning if not correctly stored at a temperature of 0°C–5°C [1] and cooked thoroughly [1]; They have a short shelf life [1]; High-risk foods include foods which are not cooked before being eaten so, if contaminated, the bacteria will not be destroyed, for example, cream, cooked meats, raw fish (for sushi), quiche [1]; Protein foods such as meat, poultry, eggs, milk and fish are high-risk foods as is cooked rice and pasta. Other high-risk foods are moist foods such as gravy, soup and unpasteurised food, for example soft cheese [1]

9.2 Ensure the probe is clean by using an antibacterial wipe before and after use [1]; Before use, make sure the probe has been calibrated and reset to 0°C [1]; Check the centre or thickest part of the chicken with the probe [1]; Check that the temperature has reached 72°C for at least 2 minutes to ensure bacteria have been killed. [1]

10.1 **Two from:** Ultra-Heat Treated (UHT) [1]; Sterilised [1]; Canned [1]

10.2 Skimmed milk is pasteurised but has had all or most of the fat removed [1]; Semi-skimmed milk is pasteurised but has had some of the fat removed. [1]

10.3 **Four from:** Soya [1]; Rice [1]; Coconut [1]; Almond [1]; Oat [1]

10.4 **Four from:** They are dairy free/100% plant based, and plant-based foods are better for the planet because

they use fewer natural resources [1]; Reducing consumption of saturated fat contributes to the maintenance of normal blood cholesterol levels [1]; Usually fortified with calcium to aid strong healthy bones [1]; They are all lactose free so suitable for those people who are intolerant to lactose (a form of sugar found in milk) [1]; They are also suitable for vegans who do not consume animal products [1]; They are usually fortified and nutrient enhanced [1]

11.1 Allows poultry or animals access to outdoor areas for part of their lives. [1]

11.2 **Three from:** More ethical [1]; Lower negative environmental impact [1]; Animals have better quality meat [1]; Egg laying hens produce more nutritious and tasty eggs [1]

11.3 **Two suitable answers, e.g.** chicken, eggs, pork, beef. [2]

11.4 **Three from:** An environment similar to intensively farmed chicken [1]; Access to natural light from windows [1]; Lower density of birds per square metre than intensively farmed chickens [1]; They have some environmental enrichment such as fresh straw. [1]

11.5 Produce is grown naturally without chemical or synthetic treatments [1]; Natural composts and manure used as fertilisers [1]; They are GM free [1]

Notes

Notes

Acknowledgements

The author and publisher are grateful to the copyright holders for permission to use quoted materials and images.

p.6-7, p.148 Bridge hold and claw grip. This resource was developed for the DfE Licence to Cook programme 2007-2011. © Crown copyright 2007. http://www.nationalarchives.gov.uk/doc/open-government-licence/version/3/

p.12 Peeling food, grating food, stirring food. This resource was developed for the DfE Licence to Cook programme 2007-2011. © Crown copyright 2007. http://www.nationalarchives.gov.uk/doc/open-government-licence/version/3/

p.28 The Eatwell Guide. © Crown Copyright 2016. Contains public sector information licensed under the Open Government Licence v3.0. http://www.nationalarchives.gov.uk/doc/open-government-licence/version/3/

p.83 © Food Standards Agency

p.99 Libby Welch / Alamy Stock Photo

p.95 Carolyn Jenkins / Alamy Stock Photo

All other images © Shutterstock.com

Every effort has been made to trace copyright holders and obtain their permission for the use of copyright material. The author and publisher will gladly receive information enabling them to rectify any error or omission in subsequent editions. All facts are correct at time of going to press.

Published by Collins
An imprint of HarperCollins*Publishers Ltd*
1 London Bridge Street
London SE1 9GF

HarperCollins*Publishers*
Macken House, 39/40 Mayor Street Upper, Dublin 1, DO1 C9W8, Ireland

© HarperCollins*Publishers* Limited 2022

This edition published 2022

ISBN 9780008535032

First published 2017

10 9 8 7 6 5 4 3 2

British Library Cataloguing in Publication Data.

A CIP record of this book is available from the British Library.

Authored by: Fiona Balding, Barbara Monks, Barbara Rathmill, Suzanne Gray and Kath Callaghan with Louise T. Davies
Contributor: Sarah Middleton
Commissioning Editors: Fiona Burns, Katherine Wilkinson and Clare Souza
Project Editor: Katie Galloway
Cover Design: Kevin Robbins and Sarah Duxbury
Inside Concept Design: Sarah Duxbury and Paul Oates
Text Design and Layout: Jouve India Private Limited
Production: Lyndsey Rogers
Printed in the UK, by Martins The Printers

Published in association with the Food Teachers Centre.